Talented Children

Identification and Education

Talented Children

Identification and Education

By

Dr. Mihir Kumar Mallick

DISCOVERY PUBLISHING HOUSE
NEW DELHI

Published by:
Tilak Wasan
DISCOVERY PUBLISHING HOUSE PVT. LTD.
4383/4B, Ansari Road, Darya Ganj
New Delhi-110 002 (India)
Phone : +91-11-23279245, 23253475, 43596065
E-mail : discoverypublishinghouse@gmail.com
sales@discoverypublishinggroup.com
web : www.discoverypublishinggroup.com

Edition: 2020

ISBN: 978-81-7141-724-7

Talented Children: *Identification and Education*

Printed at:
Infinity Imaging Systems
Delhi

Dedicated to
my
revered father
&
beloved Mother

Preface

Ober the last two decades as the mainstreaming and inclusive education movement in education has gained momentum, there has been an increase in concern for education of the children with special learning needs. Children with special learning needs require special education and related services because they are markedly different from others in one or more of the ways. They may have mental retardation, learning disabilities, disordered speech or language, impaired hearing, impaired locomotion, impaired sight, or special gifts or talents. Unfortunately, the educational needs of certain sub-groups of this population of children, i.e., "talented physically challenged children" have been slow to receive attention.

History tells us that talented individuals with handicapping conditions can make significant contributions to society, if they are given the opportunity to develop their potentials at an early age. A look at the literature states that until recent times, the gifted/talented children with handicaps were generally undereducated. Where they received special programming, if at all, it was in the area of handicap with no special provisions for nurturing gifts and talents. These children form a unique and special group whose educational interests cannot be overlooked at all.

Our legislation clearly states that children with handicapping conditions must be served. Besides, in a democracy, it is important to understand the concept of "equality of opportunity in the light of the "appropriateness of the opportunity for one and all". Failure to identify and nurture talent among the physically challenged children is unfair to them and to the society as a whole. In a developing country like India we are in need of every sort of talents that can be made available to us. These children with superior abilities are in great demand because we need them for our challenging future in various disciplines. It is felt that there has been a general neglect in providing special educational services to this unique group of children.

Gifted and talented children with handicapping conditions are generally recognised for their handicap, not for their talents. Often, their potential gifts and talents remain unnoticed in the eyes of their teachers. In the words of Maker and Grossi, the basic problem in identifying giftedness in handicapped individuals is to remove the mask that a disability can place over intellectual ability, talent and creativity. It is easy to identify individuals with an handicap such as visual impairment, speech impairment, or those who are gifted/talented. Identifying the potential gift/talent of a child who cannot speak or see or hold a pencil presents a unique problem and challenge. It is obvious to note that an early identification and appropriate educational programming for these children could release a very significant amount of creative productivity of great value to society. This would, also reduce the unnecessary waste of a great manpower.

This book attempts to explain in detail about various issues, difficulties and modern processes involved in identification of potential gifts and talents of the children with handicapping conditions. It highlights the problems and needs faced by these children. The book also documents various suggestions given for the parents, teachers and other related professionals for the purpose of proper caring and education of this neglected sub-population of children.

This book carries, in all, six chapters followed by a vivid bibliography. Each chapter starts with a brief introduction.

Chapter 1, highlights the concept of giftedness and talent. It explains in detail the characteristics and the present educational status of the talented exceptional children.

Chapter 2, shows the theoretical backdrop on which the frame work of this book is developed. It shows in detail the concept of self, its origin and development. Learning styles, types of learning styles, theories of learning styles, theories of motivation and achievement motivation have also been discussed in detail with special reference to the talented exceptional children.

Chapter 3 documents the research studies conducted on the talented physically challenged children both in India and abroad.

Chapter 4 depicts in detail the methodology employed and the procedure used for data collection. This also shows the research paradigm and the tools used.

Chapter 5 explores the status of the talented orthopaedically impaired, visually impaired and speech and hearing impaired children on perception of self, learning styles and motivational characteristics. The regression equations attempt to show the strength of predictability.

Chapter 6 comprises of the conclusions, educational implications and suggestions.

Acknowledgement

I am indebted to Professor K.K. Jain, Department of Education, University of Delhi, for his valuable guidance and suggestions, which helped me in giving the present shape of this book.

I thank the principals, teachers and students of all the four special schools of Delhi from where the sample groups were organized in assisting me in collecting data.

I express my sincere thanks to Dr. (Mrs.) Krishna Maitra, Reader, Department of Education, University of Delhi, for her valuable guidance.

I have no words to express my debt of gratitude to my parents for bearing with me all along. I am thankful to my brothers and sister for their love and affections. I shall remain indebted to my mother-in-law for her constant help. I wish to thank most sincerely my wife, Pranati, for her unending patience and support.

Dr. Mihir Kumar Mallick

Contents

1

Talented Exceptional Children—A Contextual Introduction

Introduction

Recognition of the special needs of gifted/talented children with handicapping conditions has been a very recent phenomenon even though the idea that the physically challenged individuals could possess special gifts or talents is not a new one. Historically, there have been many instances of physically challenged individuals who have made huge contributions to society from time to time. Some obvious examples include Thomas Edison, Helen Keller, and Franklin Roosevelt (Goertzel and Goertzel, 1962). Other notable people such as Albert Einstein, Woodrow Wilson, and Auguste Rodin, had learning difficulties in reading, writing and spelling (Thompson, 1971). Despite the widespread recognition of a few such individuals, we do not know how many more physically challenged individuals failed due to lack of recognition and support or inappropriate schooling.

Typically, gifted/talented children with handicaps are recognized for their handicapping conditions, not for their gifts and talents. Data regarding the number of gifted individuals with handicapping conditions are sketchy, because we fail to recognize, support and nourish their potential properly. Mouser (1980) found that 2.3% of learning disabled children were gifted. Whitmore and Maker (1985) asserted that there were no accurate statistics on the incidence of giftedness among the physically challenged but estimated conservatively that at least 2% of the physically challenged children are intellectually gifted. However, it has been estimated that, between 2 to 5 per cent of children with handicapping conditions are gifted/talented only with the exceptions of mental retardation. On the basis of the above stated data, it is believed that there are as many gifted/talented individuals among the physically challenged individuals as in any other segment of the population.

To determine the status of the education of the talented physically challenged children, we are struck with the realization that a very little work has been done to serve this group. In the past, gifted/talented children with handicaps were grossly under-served. Though slowly and steadily only a few isolated programs came to exist for education of these children. But these cases were very rare. Johnson and Corn (1989), report that only few individuals who had the support of informed, concerned families and/or visionary innovative educators were able to develop their potential talents. Many educators have expressed their concern for the talented exceptional children depicting that a large pool of such individuals exist whose potential gifts and talents are hidden within educational settings focussed on their handicaps and they are not receiving appropriate educational services for the better utilization of their potential gifts and talents. No doubt, this segment of our population is vastly under-served and neglected.

Failure to identify and nurture giftedness/talent among the physically challenged individuals is unfair to them and to society at large. The basic tenet of any educational endeavour is that all individuals must be given opportunities to maximize their potentials. Moreover, failing to actualize one's potential creates a breeding ground for frustration and poor mental health. As a society we are badly in need of all sorts of talents that can be made available to us. Failure to identify and serve the gifted/talented physically challenged children is an indictment against our constitution and gross violation of human rights.

Legislation clearly states that children with handicaps must be served. With regard to educational provisions of the physically challenged children, the persons with disabilities (Equal Opportunities, Protection of Rights and Full Participation) act

1995, which came into existence on 1st January, 1996, documents that:

I. The appropriate governments and the local authorities shall:

- *(a)* ensure that every child with a disability has access to free education in an appropriate environment till he attains the age of eighteen years;
- *(b)* endeavour to promote the integration of students with disabilities in the normal schools;
- *(c)* promote setting up of special schools in government and private sector for those in need of special education in such a manner that children with disabilities living in any part of the country have access to such schools;
- *(d)* endeavour to equip the special schools for children with disabilities with vocational training facilities.

II. The appropriate governments and the local authorities shall by notification make schemes for:

- *(a)* conducting part-time classes in respect of children with disabilities who having completed education up to class fifth and could not continue their studies on a whole-time basis;
- *(b)* conducting special part-time classes for providing functional literacy for children in the age group of sixteen and above;
- *(c)* imparting non-formal education by utilizing the available manpower in rural areas after giving them appropriate orientation;
- *(d)* imparting education through open schools or open universities;
- *(e)* conducting class and discussions through interactive electronic or other media; and
- *(f)* providing every child with disability free of cost special books and equipments needed for his education.

III. Without prejudice to the foregoing provisions, the appropriate governments shall by notification prepare a comprehensive education scheme which shall make provision for:

(a) transport facilities to the children with disabilities or in the alternative financial incentives to parents or guardians to enable their children with disabilities to attend schools;

(b) the removal of architectural barriers from schools, colleges or other institutions imparting vocational and professional training;

(c) the supply of books, uniforms and other materials to children with disabilities attending schools;

(d) the grant of scholarship to students with disabilities;

(e) setting up of appropriate fora for the redressal of grievances of parents regarding the placement of their children with disabilities;

(f) suitable modification in the examination system to eliminate purely mathematical questions for the benefit of blind students and students with low vision;

(g) restructuring of curriculum for the benefit of children with disabilities;

(h) restructuring of curriculum for benefit of students with hearing impairment to facilitate them to take only one language as part of their curriculum.

IV. All educational institutions shall provide or cause to be provided amanuensis to blind students and students with low vision.

Over the last few years, the pioneers of gifted education have started giving importance on the education of the gifted/talented physically challenged children. By the early eighties, education of gifted physically challenged children was being hailed as a "new frontier" (Whitmore, 1981), and educators were being challenged to develop procedures for identifying creative potential in handicapped children (Ford and Ford, 1981) to make appropriate use of new technology in the classroom (Higgins, 1981), and to provide appropriate individual educational programs which could encourage development of potential while attending to the areas of deficit (Karnes, Schwedel, and Linnerneyer, 1982). Whitmore and Maker (1985) stated that, "appropriate educational programming for the gifted handicapped children could release a very significant amount of creative productivity of great value to society and would also reduce the possibility of economic dependence in adult years". In the views of Gallagher (1988), "gifted physically challenged as one target group should be given top priority". Despite this early flurry of professional interest and high sounding slogans, unfortunately, attention to gifted/talented physically challenged children has been neglected in our country.

Concept of Giftedness and Talent

The term "giftedness" and "talent" are used interchangeably in literature over the ages. Definitions of gifted and talented have become more inclusive. In the words of Marland (1972), "Gifted and talented children are those identified by professionally qualified persons who, by virtue of outstanding abilities, are capable of high performance. Children capable of high performance include those with demonstrated achievement and/or potential ability in any of the following areas singly or in combination:

(i) general intellectual ability;

(ii) specific academic aptitude;

(iii) creative or productive thinking;

(iv) leadership ability;

(v) visual and performing arts; and

(vi) psychomotor ability".

Renzulli (1978) defines giftedness as "an interaction among three basic clusters of human traits—these clusters being above average general abilities, high levels of task commitment and high levels of creativity". Many authors have attempted to define giftedness and talent in numerous ways. A look at those definitions state that many of them associate giftedness with intellectual ability and talent with an non-intellectual ability such as artistic, technical or athletic skills.

Gagne (1985), while differentiating giftedness from talent states that "giftedness corresponds to competence that is distinctly above average in one or more domains of human aptitude and talent corresponds to performance that is distinctly above average in one or more fields of human activity". According to Gagne (1985), giftedness refers to natural abilities, or aptitudes while talent represents one's developed abilities or skills. Gagne (1985), divides aptitudes (gifts) into four categories i.e. intellectual, creative, socio-affective and sensori-motor and talents into five categories, namely, academic, technical, artistic, interpersonal and athletic which has been shown in the following diagram. (p. 7)

Gagne's above stated model carries three components namely:

(*a*) gift components,

(*b*) catalysts components,

(*c*) talent components.

(a) Gift Components

Gagne proposes four gifts expressed in terms of aptitudes namely, intellectual, creative, socio-affective, and sensori-motor. The intellectual domain represents specific abilities like verbal, spatial, numerical, perceptual, mechanical, and mnemonic ability. The creative domain not only includes the creative aptitudes like fluency, flexibility, originality and elaboration as proposed by Guilford and Torrance, but also encompasses on certain personality traits like sense of humour, curiosity, artistic interests or talent, tolerance for ambiguity, spontaneity etc.

The socio-affective domain represents the social aptitudes of an individual. The sensori-motor domain focuses on abilities related to the various senses, precision, and speed of visuo-motor coordination, gross motor abilities (strength, speed, flexibility, etc.), balance or kinesthetic abilities and so forth.

(b) Catalysts Component

The catalysts act as positive or negative moderators that transform aptitudes into talents. Gagne recognizes two types of catalysts: intrapersonal and environmental. The intrapersonal domain comprises various psychological traits of an individual like curiosity, motivation, perseverance, autonomy etc. Gagne states aptitudes are involved as constituent elements of talents, whereas the catalysts provide a frame-work that supports the

THE DIFFERENTIATED GIFTEDNESS–TALENT MODEL BY–GAGNE (1985)

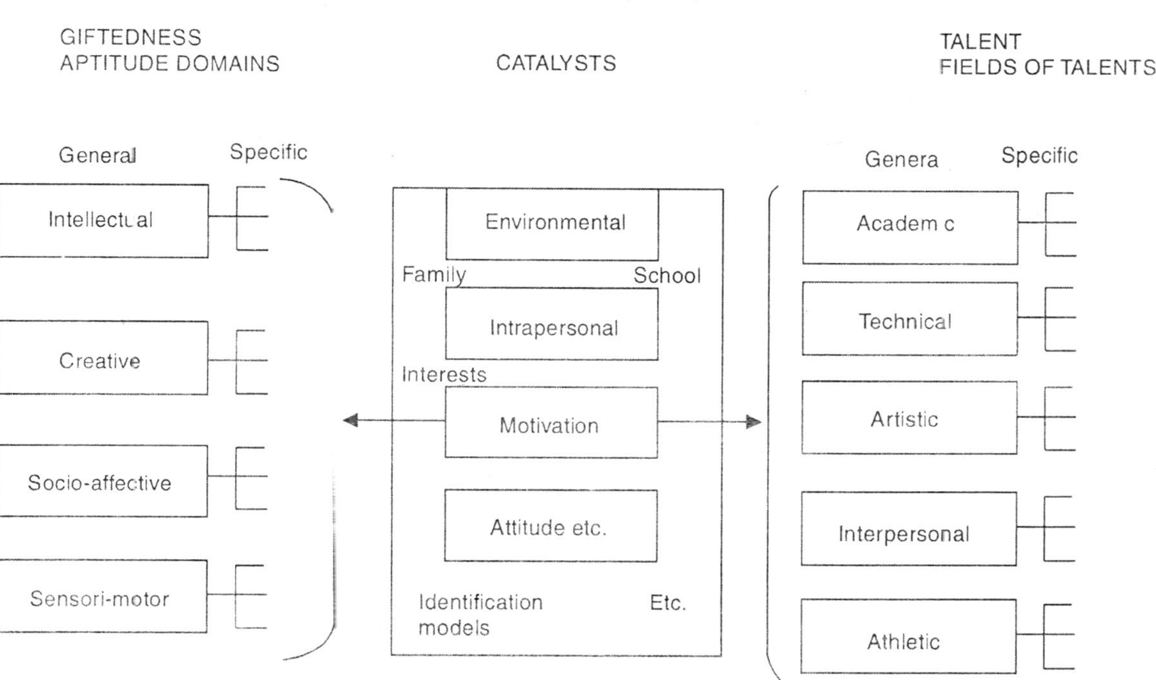

development of talents. Two intrapersonal catalysts seem to play a particularly important role: interest and motivation. Interests help steer a person toward a field of talent in which his or her energies will be invested, while motivation determines how much energy will be applied to learning activities in the chosen field of talent. The environmental domain represents the roles of parents, siblings, peers, schools etc.

(c) Talent Component

The talent component contains five general categories of talent: academic, technical, interpersonal, artistic, and athletic domains. The academic domain reflects one's talent in literature, social science, mathematics, science etc. and the technical domain represents one's abilities in various trades. The artistic domain represents one's talent in visual arts, crafts, drama, music, singing, dance etc. The interpersonal domain focuses on one's ability in leadership trait, administration, and public dealings etc., while athletic domain focuses on one's ability in games and sports.

According to Gagne, talents stem from the interaction between aptitudes that are necessarily above average but not necessarily exceptional, and the facilitating action of the intrapersonal and environmental catalysts. The dynamics between them is represented by the following equation:

$$T = f(A \times C)$$

[T= talent; A= Aptitude (gift); C= Catalyst]

Gagne reports that each specific talent is expressed by a particular profile of aptitudes, somewhat different from the profile characteristic of any other talent and each aptitude may contribute to the development of many distinct talents. The above stated model states that where there is a talent there necessarily is a set of underlying aptitudes, whether or not they are visible to the untrained eye. No matter what the talent, it must find its source in one or probably, several aptitudes. On the other hand, a gift is not necessarily actualized in a specific field of talent. Level of skill in an aptitude or in a talent is a normative concept; thus, there is no absolute threshold of talent. One becomes talented insofar as one's performance is well above average in a reference population, whatever the size of population would be.

Definition of Talented Exceptional Children

The term exceptional children refers to "those who require special education and related services if they are to realize their full human potential". These children require special education because they are markedly different from most children in one or more of the following ways. They may have mental retardation, learning disabilities, disordered speech or language, impaired hearing, impaired locomotion, impaired sight, or special gifts or talents. Most exceptional individuals have a disability, and they are often referred as "handicapped" in everyday conversation.

Because of their handicapping conditions, they need specially designed instructions for the purpose of their education. In modern terminology these individuals are known as group of children with special learning needs and are best known as "physically challenged children".

Though there are various categories of exceptional children, the present study has focussed only on the talented orthopaedically impaired, visually impaired and speech and hearing impaired children.

While defining "talented exceptional children", the researcher has attempted to explain the term "talent" in terms of giftedness. A broadly accepted definition on "gifted handicapped" states that the gifted handicapped are those individuals of exceptional ability or potential who can achieve high performance, despite handicap such as hearing, visual, or orthopaedic impairment, emotional disturbance or learning disabilities".

Current definitions of giftedness which acknowledge multifaceted manifestations of high potential are more amenable to the conceptualization of gifted handicapped than the more stringent traditional definitions based only on high I.Q. scores. The definition proposed by Marland (1972) has been found influential in broadening the concept of giftedness to include children with handicaps. According to Marland (1972), "gifted and talented children are those identified by professionally qualified persons who, by virtue of outstanding abilities, are capable of high performance. These children require differentiated educational programs and services beyond those normally provided by the regular school program in order to realize their potential contribution to self and society".

Children capable of high performance include those with demonstrated achievement/or potential ability in any of the following areas:

- General intellectual ability;
- Specific academic aptitude,
- Creative of productive thinking,
- Leadership ability, and
- Visual and performing arts,
- Psychomotor ability.

Following the above said definition, a child does not have to be superior in all dimensions in order to be considered talented. High potential or demonstrated achievement in only one area is sufficient to meet the criteria of giftedness. A child with a severe handicap, like any other child, could then meet the criteria for giftedness, by showing high potential or performance in at least one of the above said six areas.

The term "talented exceptional children" in the present study refers to "those physically challenged children who demonstrate potential gifts or talents in any, some or all of the areas mentioned i.e. (i) general intellectual abilities, (ii) specific academic aptitudes, (iii) creative productive thinking, (iv) leadership ability, (v) visual and performing arts, and (vi) psychomotor ability".

In order to have better understanding of the term talented exceptional children, it could be said that a talented exceptional child requires special educational services for one or more areas of potential giftedness, and for one or more types of handicapping conditions. These children do form an extreme heterogeneous group, with great variability of individual profiles of strengths and weaknesses.

Characteristics of the Talented Exceptional Children

Gifted/talented exceptional children manifest a variety of both positive and negative characteristics. Friedrichs (1990) states that positive qualities may be interpreted in a negative way by adults working with these children. According to Whitmore (1981), Whitmore and Maker (1985), the positive characteristics possessed by the gifted/talented exceptional children are:

- superior memory and general knowledge;
- superior analysis and creative problem solving skills;
- notable drive to know or master;
- superior use of language—oral or written;
- exceptional comprehension;
- keen sense of humour;
- persistence in pursuit of academic or intellectual tasks,
- awareness and/or ability to capitalize to their handicapped peers in visual and performing art, music, drama, dance, leadership trait, and in sports etc.

These individuals, in general, have a positive vision of their potential accurate self knowledge of their strengths, and high degree of energy in trying to reach their goals (Whitmore and Maker, 1985, Wingenbach, 1985). Successful gifted physically challenged individuals have been observed to have an intense drive to succeed in realizing their goals. They are capable of devising creative coping strategies for goal attainments. These have shown to include strategies for overcoming personal limitations (Whitmore and Maker, 1985), and alternative solutions for attainment of a goal (Robertson, 1985).

Yewchuk and Bibby (1989a) report that the characteristics of giftedness which teachers perceive in physically challenged children have been found to be very similar to those perceived in non-handicapped children. Severely and profoundly talented hearing impaired children are found to possess superior recall, expressive ability, eagerness to learn and keen observation. Talented hearing impaired children, like their counterparts, excel in intellectual, academic and motivational endeavours to their peers.

The negative characteristics associated with the gifted/talented exceptional children as reported by - Meisgeier and Werblo (1978); Neilson and Mortorff-Albert (1989), Vespi and Yewchuk (1992), Whitmore and Maker (1985) are:

- Fragile self-concept,
- Struggle with self acceptance,
- Feelings of social discomfort and shame,
- A need to release or vent pent-up energies,
- Interpersonal difficulties with peers, teachers, and family,
- Academic difficulties in selected skill areas etc.

Schiff, Kaufman and Kaufman (1981) report that for some individuals these negative characteristics may develop into emotional/behavioural difficulties. Others may become socially isolated, either through withdrawn or aggressive behaviour (Meisgeier, Meisgeier, and Werblo, 1978). An end-result might involve avoidance of academic and social involvement because of the fear of rejection.

Biereley (1991) reports that part of the emotional difficulties faced by gifted handicapped individuals may lie in the conflicting patterns typically observed in handicapped and in gifted individuals in the areas of control, field dependence/ independence, achievement-motivation and learned helplessness. The talented exceptional children tend to respond according to the more independent adult pattern than their peers; they show internal control, field independence, and expectation of success. The deaf and congenitally blind children tend to show more dependent externally controlled behaviour. In situations where talented/gifted physically challenged individuals are treated as handicapped persons to the neglect of their intellectual ability and talents. Biereley (1991) assumes that a "handicapped" pattern is likely to emerge, but in a proper environment, the "gifted pattern" could emerge.

According to Friedrichs (1990), the positive qualities of the talented exceptional children may not appear praiseworthy to adults around them. For instance, these students might aspire to negative goals, such as identifying and criticizing inconsistent school practices. Many times these children experience painful results because of the interaction of positive and negative characteristics. According to Whitmore (1981), Tannenbaum and Baldwin (1983), and Friedrichs (1990), the handicapped children with potential gift and talent are found to possess school adjustment problems, feelings of exclusion, inner conflicts, uneven profile, frustration, and fragile self-concept. The talented exceptional children possess a fear of failure associated with the discrepancy between high expectations based on self-perceptions of abilities and low achievement resulting from the disability.

Pledgie (1982) reports various learning and motivational characteristics of the talented/gifted physically challenged children:

- They have advanced, expressive and elaborate vocabulary, and may read prior to school entry;
- They memorize and recall information easily;
- They are aware of cause and effect relationships and can question and apply information;
- Engage in divergent thinking; can generalize and provide more than one correct answer;
- They have a prolonged attention and are persistent;
- They are curious, have many interests, and may be high risk takers;
- They generally display a sense of humor;

Talented exceptional children are found being rejected by others, labelled low achievers by teachers and feel less capable many times. As a result they develop poor self-concept.

Talented Exceptional Children—An Educational Perspective

It is a known fact that we are lagging behind in developing appropriate procedure for identifying and programming for talented/gifted children with handicapping conditions. A general neglect has been experienced so far as education of this sub-population is concerned. Karnes (1989) attributes this neglect to a lack of coordinated leadership arising from the separation of education services for gifted/talented physically challenged students. Teachers of the physically challenged children are not properly trained to recognize potential gifts or talents as well as are unaware of services for this sub-population.

From Gallagher's (1989) perspective, the neglect may be attributed to both administrative and logistical psychological barriers. To Hanninen (1989), the emphasis within special education programs on the handicapping condition rather than on serving the whole child has contributed to the neglect of potential giftedness or talent. Where the handicapping condition is very superior, teachers consider the development of basic skills so important that other considerations, including encouragement of gifts and talents are relegated to a position of secondary importance.

However, Colangelo and Davis (1991) document the following factors in "Handbook of Gifted Education" which hinder in identifying and developing appropriate educational programs for the gifted/talented children with handicapping conditions:

(a) **Inappropriate Identification Procedures:** One difficulty in identifying the talented exceptional children is expecting these children to demonstrate the same characteristics as possessed by the non-handicapped talented children. Instruments used in identifying the talented physically challenged children are not appropriate. The procedure of identifying these children on a one-time basis is faulty. Because, these children have not had the opportunity to fully develop their potential and to explore their potential gifts. Standardized tests which could be used for identification purpose are found to be very limited.

(b) **Faulty Expectations:** Teachers and parents of this sub-group of population have high expectations. Whitmore and Maker (1985) point out that some of the expectations of typical gifted children may impede identification of the talented handicapped. For example some normal gifted are expected to "look bright", while some physically challenged children who are very bright may look dull. Some physically challenged children do not display curiosity by physically investigating the environment, as is typical of many gifted children. At the same time Whitmore and Maker (1985) explain that "the most important needs that can be met by both educators and families are high expectations for success and an environment that facilitates achievement". Expectations must be within capabilities of the child. Showing confidence in the child's ability to produce and supporting his or her efforts will bring about positive results.

(c) **Developmental Delays:** Handicapping conditions restrict the attainment of different developmental tasks. Maker (1977) reports that the cognitive development and intellectual functioning of a child may delay when certain handicapping conditions prevent the child's ability to respond to cognitive stimulation to demonstrate cognitive abilities through expression and problem solving. Therefore, in many cases gifts/talents appear slowly. However, adequate encouragement, support and appropriate programming could help these children to prosper their potential gifts or talents.

(d) **Gaps in Information:** Identification of the talented exceptional children involves gathering of information regarding the developmental characteristics of these children from various sources like parents, teachers, counsellors, psychologists and other related professionals. Gaps in such information stand as a barrier in identifying them which adversely affect the educational placement and programming.

(e) **Lack of Professional Training:** Special educators working in the field are poorly equipped to identify and educate the talented physically challenged children. Many of them may have little or no knowledge about characteristics of these children. On the other hands professionals in gifted education have little knowledge about handicaps or the effects of a handicapping condition on learning. Besides, the mainstreamed educators often have had formal training in either the handicapped or in the gifted areas.

(f) **Lack of Appropriate Counselling:** Whitmore and Maker (1985) report that the school system does very little to promote the development of the talented/gifted physically challenged children. They fail to receive the kind of counselling they need because of which they do not actualize their potential gift/talents. In many cases they are deprived of career counselling. These children need to have an opportunity to explore different careers, to know their strengths, and special abilities, and to match career goals with interests and capabilities. Unfortunately our special schools hereby do not provide facilities that would help the talented exceptional children to grow in the line of their potential gifts/ talents and to bring substantial success to mankind.

(g) **Curriculum and Instruction:** The content of the curriculum and the instructional mode typically found in special educational programmes are often inappropriate for the development of these children's intellect. In regular elementary classrooms, they are often placed in the low ability groups, and taught in a style appropriate for slow learners. On the other hand, in special education classes, children are trained in self-help skills, but are not given encouragement or guidance in learning to develop their mental abilities. As a consequence it has not been uncommon for the physically challenged pupils to be overlooked as gifted because of the lack of opportunity to observe their higher intellectual abilities. There is a general lack of higher academic achievement among these children due to limitations in their ability to learn and to produce the quantity of work at the pace typical of high achievers. Most teachers of the physically challenged children are not trained to look for, stimulate, or develop the intellectual independence of the talented physically challenged children.

Need of the Study

The Proponents of gifted education from time to time have stated that the talented physically challenged children are deprived of appropriate special educational facilities and related services. These children continue to be ignored, programs for them are lacking, and their problems are compounded as severe social problems. We cannot continue to ignore our obligation to the physically challenged individuals who are potentially gifted/talented. For the good of our society and for well-being of the talented physically challenged children, we must put forth greater effort to alleviate the problems of under-serving of these children.

A look at the literature depicts that over the last two decades very little research has been conducted on talented exceptional children. With few exceptions most researches have been conducted with adults who are gifted and also handicapped (Maker, Radden, Tonelson, and Howell, 1978). Out of all researches conducted on the gifted/talented exceptional children, the gifted learning-disabled children have received most attention (Karness and Johnson, 1991). There has been very little research conducted on the effectiveness of interventions with this group of children. Karnes and Johnson (1991), in the "Handbook of Gifted Education (1991, Pa-431)", reports that "relatively few models that others might want to adopt have been developed and tested. Likewise, we have a dearth of research findings to endorse or refute the interventions that have been developed and disseminated. When there are no research models or research work to guide practice, educators often do not know what to do with this neglected group. Critical questions must be answered by carefully designed research".

Whitmore and Maker (1985) while depicting the case studies of gifted hearing impaired, visually impaired, physically handicapped and learning disabled children in their book, "Intellectually Giftedness in Disable Persons", stated that "each gifted handicapped child is unique and they can be dealt effectively following separate guidelines". Many of the pioneers of gifted education have asserted that, the gifted physically challenged children have traits and characteristics which make them fundamentally different from the general run of humanity. They learn, perceive, think and adjust in ways which are unique to them and they cannot be understood in terms of those principles of learning, thinking, perceiving and adjusting which have been derived from and applicable to normal children". Hence it is obvious to note that, the talented physically challenged children do perceive their abilities, worth, beliefs, and thoughts etc., in unique ways which would contribute later in building up their self-concept. Since, these children are deprived of many of the sensory inputs, they adopt different approaches in learning tasks and solving problems. At the same time motivation, an important psychological factor would energize them to achieve goals of life by adopting various means which are generally different from the normal ones.

Researches conducted in the field of gifted/talented exceptional children document that, most of them are found repetitive, and have focussed on I.Q. or intellectual functioning as an indicator of giftedness. Researchers have attempted to study mostly "self-concept" and in few cases "motivation" of the gifted/talented children with handicaps. Many research findings suggest that I.Q. or intellectual ability of this sub-group of children could be not only considered in determining the potential gift/talent. They argue that, standardized psychological tools are of limited use because they lack norms which could be used and applicable to the physically challenged children. Another notable factor that many of the physically challenged children like visually impaired and speech and hearing impaired lack are vision and language respectively, because of which they do experience a delay in cognitive development, which consequently affect their intellectual functioning. Similarly in case of the orthopaedically impaired children, a late entry to school has been found very common. Therefore, these children are not always at par with their normal age peers with regard to intellectual abilities. Professionals of gifted education have always suggested to develop research based tools for the identification of the gifted/talented physically challenged children focusing on the areas other then intellectual functioning. The researcher felt motivated to take up a study which could help him develop suitable tools for identifying the talent/giftedness of the physically challenged children as well as to answer many unanswered question like:

(a) How do various categories of talented exceptional children perceive their beliefs, thoughts, values, worth, goals, abilities, and potentialities that could reflect their "perception of self"?

(b) What are the approaches the talented exceptional children do adopt in learning tasks and solving

problems, which could be better explained in terms of their "learning styles"?

(c) What is the type of motivational characteristics that talented exceptional children do possess?

Hardly, any study has been conducted either in India or abroad on gifted/talented physically challenged children focusing on major affective variables, namely, "perception of self", "learning styles", and "motivational characteristics", and their combined effect. It is, in this context, that the researcher has taken up the study entitled, "A study of talented exceptional children in relation to their perception of self, learning styles and motivational characteristics" so as to create concrete help and guidance to future planners, psychologists, counsellors, and educators of special schools whose numbers are going to swell tremendously in coming years.

Statement of the Problem

"A study of talented exceptional children in relation to their perception of self, learning styles and motivational characteristics".

Objectives of the Study

1. To identify the talented orthopaedically impaired, visually impaired and speech and hearing impaired children.
2. To explore the perception of self, learning styles and motivational characteristics of the talented orthopaedically impaired, visually impaired and speech and hearing impaired children.
3. To explore the differences among each of the three groups of talented exceptional children on the above said three variables.
4. To find out inter-correlations among perception of self, learning styles, and motivational characteristics of each of the three groups of talented exceptional children.
5. To find out strength of predictability of teacher's perception of each of the three groups of talented exceptional children on the basis of perception of self, learning styles, and motivational characteristics.

6. To find out strength of predictability of perception of self of each of the three groups of talented exceptional children on the basis of learning styles and motivational characteristics.

Definition of the Important Terms

1. **The self:** The term self in its literary sense refers to a particular individual, that is, a personality we wish to single out from the rest of human mankind. It is a term referring to a specific person and has been indispensable in the historical development of person as conscious and thinking entity. Description of the characteristics and attributes of a particular self is more complex and a self can be observed from innumerable frames of reference. To have a better understanding of the term "self", it can be described as the description an individual makes about his/her own. Each person possesses a large number of such ways of describing and distinguishing himself/herself as unique among other people. An individual in the process of development develops a variety of selves. Among them social self, physical self, and academic self are considered as important ones in developing a global self-concept.

    (a) **Social self:** This is the aspect of self, "as perceived by an individual in relation to others", but pertains to "others" in general way. It reflects a child's sense of adequacy and worth in social interaction. It also explores a child's perception of his/her behaviour, moral worth, and feelings of being right or wrong, good or bad.

    (b) **Physical self:** This aspect of self of a child reflects one's views about his/her body, state of health, physical appearance, skills and sexuality. It also pertains to child's sense of personal worth, feeling of adequacy as a person, and the evaluation of his or her personality apart from the body or the relationship to others. In general it tells about one's body image.

    (c) **Academic self:** The academic self, broadly known as academic self-concept, reflects a child's perceived worth and abilities in academic endeavour. It explores a child's perception about failure and success, preferences for various subjects, perception about his or her ability and future performance, dependence or independence in the matter of study or work habits and above all academic ability.

2. **Learning Styles:** The term "learning style" generally refers to learner's characteristic approach to learning. In literature it has been used in two distinct ways:

   (i) It has been used to indicate a broad description of relatively consistent behaviour related to ways of going about learning; it is treated as individual difference of generality comparable to intelligence and personality, but describing consistency in the ways people tackle learning tasks.

   (ii) The definition has been narrowed considerably to parallel the idea of cognitive style, with the use of bipolar traits, but described in relation to the learning tasks commonly found in education contexts, as opposed to scores on psychological tests. In both senses, the term attempts to cover a range of concepts which have emerged from attempts to describe aspects of student's learning. However, in the present study the second approach as explained above has been taken into account in studying student's learning style and the most widely accepted concept on learning style as conceived by D.A. Kolb (1976) has been strictly followed. Thus the term learning style used in the present study has been borrowed from Kolb's work, which states "learning style is a result of heredity, experience and present environment, and each one's learning style is a combination of four basic learning modes, namely, concrete experience, reflective observation, abstract conceptualization, and active experimentation.

3. **Motivation:** The concept of motivation does not reflect a single term or meaning and has been used in literature interchangeably with terms like internal urge, aspiration, need, motive, drive and desire etc. The term includes a number of factors governing it, a particular pattern of behaviour and a relationship among these factors. The term motivation broadly encompasses (i) the force or capacity that

energizes one's behaviour, (ii) the directionality of behaviour; i.e. effort being expanded in particular direction to achieve a goal or objective, and (iii) persistence of directional behaviour till the goal or objective is achieved. Broadly speaking the term motivation could be defined as contemporary influence on the direction, vigour and persistence of one's actions. In the present study three forms of motivation, namely, achievement motivation, task motivation, and unrelated motivation though have been studied, focus has been given on achievement motivation.

The term 'achievement motivation' attempts to account for the determinants of the direction, magnitude, and persistence of behaviour in a limited but very important domain of human activities. The motive to achieve is learned from a wide range of mastery experiences which are accompanied by strong positive affect. Once it is developed the disposition is considered to be relatively stable and is assumed to be aroused when the person expects that a situation offers the possibility of mastery and accompanying positive effect.

Delimitations of the Study

The present study has been delimited to:

1. the territory of Delhi only.
2. the special schools of Delhi.
3. the following sub-population of talented:
    - *(a)* orthopaedically impaired children.
    - *(b)* visually impaired children.
    - *(c)* speech and hearing impaired children only.

2

Conceptual Framework

Exceptional individuals constitute a separate and in many ways distinct categories or classes of people. How an individual with handicapping conditions defines himself or herself is a function of, and constructed through, interaction. People come to see them as visually impaired, mentally retarded, orthopaedically impaired, speech and hearing impaired or emotionally disturbed depending upon the nature of the handicap. Whether the physically challenged individuals are ashamed or proud of their condition or they feel neutral about is mediated by significant others like parents, teachers, peers, attendants, and others who enter their lives in social interaction. They interpret other's gestures and actions in attempting to see themselves as others see them and thereby construct the concept of self. Individuals with handicapping conditions possess particular personality characteristics and ways of thinking about themselves. For some, handicapping conditions determine how they see themselves, while for others, it is an insignificant part of how and what they think.

The psychology of such individuals differs from the normal ones both in degrees and kind. These individuals learn, perceive, think and adjust in ways which are unique to them. They cannot be studied in terms of those principles of learning, thinking, perceiving and adjusting which have been derived from, and applicable to normal ones. A separate set of conceptual strategies is required to understand and deal with the exceptional individuals particularly those who are talented exceptional ones.

This chapter is an attempt to build up a theoretical backdrop of the study with reference to self, its development, various facets of self, learning style and its types and motivational characteristics. A special reference has been given to the population of the present study.

Self—Its Origin, Development and Various Facets

Human beings have always behaved in terms of some kind of understanding of the self. In the behavioural sciences, the use of the concept of self has been often questioned. "Self" has traditionally been given an important place in formulations regarding the nature of the individual and the character of social interaction.

The concept of "self" has its origin in the prehistory of personality theory. The writings of Allport (1943, 1955, 1961), Ansbacher and Ansbacher (1956), Maslow (1956, 1954), Snygg and Combs (1949), G. Murphy (1947), Rogers (1947), Lecky (1961), and Raimy (1971), emphasied the importance of self in psychology and laid the foundation of further research.

The word "self", in its literary sense, refers to a particular individual that is a personality we wish to single out from the rest of human mankind. It is a term referring to a specific person and has been indispensable in the historical development of person as conscious and thinking entities. Description of the characteristics and attributes of a particular self is more complex, and a self can be observed from innumerable frames of reference. In the views of Combs and Soper (1957), Norman and Ainsworth (1954), Bertocci (1945), and Mead (1934), a self may be described from the point of view of any number of people, including the individual himself.

The ways in which a self may be described are particularly limitless. In order to avoid confusion and to have a proper understanding of the concept of "self" it is thought to explain the term in a precise way. The term "self" can be described as the description an individual makes about his own, for example, an individual may see himself as a man, or woman, a child or adult, a black or white, a teacher or actor etc. Each person possesses a large number of such ways of describing and distinguishing himself as unique among other people.

The perception of self doesn't stop with description alone. People perceive themselves in terms of values, for example, people regard themselves as successful or unsuccessful, as attractive or ugly, as pleasant or unpleasant, as fat or thin, as adequate or inadequate, or in terms of a thousand other descriptions of greater or lesser degree of value or importance.

The different ways in which a person perceives himself vary in the degree of centrality and of clarity. Some self-perceptions appear to be much more central or basic to everybody. For example, the concept of man and woman is usually related to the very core of our being. The self is differentiated with greater clarity throughout one's life.

Whatever be one's way of describing of one self, each person develops a large number of more or less discrete perceptions of self which he/she regards as characteristics of his/her being. They include all perceptions a person has differentiated as descriptive of what he calls 'I' or 'me' (Balester, 1956, Adler, 1951, Mc quitty, 1950, Bertocci, 1945). These perceptions don't exist in the perceptual field as a simple enumeration of ways of seeing the self. Rather, the concepts of self constitute an organization representing a person's own conception of himself in all his complexity. This organization is not a mere conglomeration of isolated concepts of self, but a patterned interrelationship or Gestalt of self-perceptions, (Combs 1958, Mead, 1934). It is the person one feels one is.

The perceptual field includes all of a person's perceptions, including those about himself and those about things outside himself. The perceptions of self irrespective of their significance in a particular situation represent the "phenomenal self" of an individual. Or, in other words, it could be said that the phenomenal self is always a self in a given situation.

To describe the organization of the central perceptions of self involved in a great deal of person's behaviour, it is necessary to differentiate from the total perceptual field those perceptions about self which seem most vital to understand an individual. This organization or set of perceptions is known as "self-concept".

The term "self-concept" as defined in the "International Encyclopedia of Education" (1985), refers "to the experience of one's own being which includes what people come to know about themselves through experience, reflection, and feedback from others. The self-concept is an organized cognitive structure comprising of a set of attitudes, beliefs, and values that cut across all facets of experience and action, organizing and tying together the variety of specific habits, abilities, outlooks, ideas, and feelings that a person displays".

In the language of "Encyclopedia of Psychology, 1994, the term "self-concept" is explained as "an organized configuration of perceptions of the self which are admissible to awareness. It is composed of such elements as the perceptions of one's characteristics, and abilities; the precepts and concepts of self in relation to others and the environment, the value qualities which are perceived as associated with experiences and objects, and goals and ideas which are perceived as having positive and negative valence."

The term self-concept serves as a kind of shorthand approach by which a person may symbolize and reduce his own vast complexity to workable and usable terms. It represents the most stable, important and characteristic self-perceptions of a person. The self-concept of a person could be used as a convenient device for understanding a person. It acts as a particular kind of attitudinal structure. The self-concept is for the most part a coherent and internally consistent cognitive system. The self-concept is the very essence of "me" whose loss is regarded as a personal destruction. Whatever the self-concept would be for an individual, it forms the very core of one's personality. However, the self-concept is the perception at all times and in all situations.

The development of self follows very much the same course that occurs with the development of other kinds of cognitive concepts. Like other system of cognitive organization the self-concept tends to be self sustaining and once it is evolved it tends to guide selectively the admissions of new experiences or new information into conceptual category. The concept of self develops gradually from the time an infant discovers the parts of his/her own body, and it is built up through thoughts, feelings and actions. Erickson's view on human development helps to set the stage for perceiving the self as being a continuous process. The first items of information which comprise the concept are associated together because of various kinds of similarity or relatedness. The early information of self-concept is especially crucial in that it guides or steers the subsequent development of self-concept.

Many factors contribute to the development of self. Overall, it is related to the scope of experiences one accumulates of oneself. It is, at first, a simplistic awareness of oneself and one's capacities generalized across all situations, but as one grows older, the self-concept becomes more complex and differentiated into sub-facets that have to do with the self in different situations as the "social self", the "academic self" and the "physical self".

Among the many forces that help to organize this accumulated experience with oneself, four are especially notable; which are language, personal success and failure; social interaction and feedback, and (physical) body image and personal identification.

Language, enables one to label experiences and actions, organizing experiences into integrated conceptual categories. Some of the earliest in the child's vocabulary have to do with the self and the physical body. Soon the child begins to label things and people that are especially important extensions of him/her (mama, dady, toy etc.). Slowly the child learns to label thoughts and actions with various evaluative terms like good, bad, naughty, nice and so on. These labels facilitate organization of experiences pertaining to the self. Language plays an important role though for everybody, particularly for individuals with speech and hearing impairment in developing self-concept. The speech and hearing impaired children lack the requisite sensory organs that enable them to communicate with the normal ones, because of which they tend to develop poor self-concept, though not all of them.

The forces of **personal success and failure,** also influence one's perception of self. Personal success and failure involve ideas and feelings arising out of rewards and punishment. The pleasure and satisfaction that accompany personal success become cognitively associated with all activities and experiences accompanying such situations, including perception of self.

Attainment of self-set goals; improvement over past performance, or measuring up to one's own standards all contribute to the consolidation of self-concept and self-esteem.

Social interaction is found to be one important factor in contributing for developing the self. As developed in the writings of Cooley and Mead, the basic position holds that the person's self-conceptions are initially developed from the views taken toward him by significant others in his social environment. Through a process of assuming imaginatively the attitudes of others toward himself, the individual eventually incorporates what he feels to be the general view of others toward him. One achieves a concept of himself by assuming the role of another person, stepping into his shoes, so to speak, to have a look back at oneself. At first one is particularly likely to view himself as he thinks he is viewed by particular individuals who are especially important or meaningful to him, such as parents, teachers or other loved or respected figures. Mead (1934) described this process of attempting to perceive oneself as he perceived by important others as assuming the role of significant others. Later, Mead suggested the individual develops a composite notion, synthesized from his interactions with many people over a range of time, to evolve a highly generalized conception of others. The ideas of Mead afterwards have been verified by empirical researches.

At any moment a person may be living in a family, school, community, religious, racial, regional, national or world subculture. The demands made on a person by these various subcultures may differ widely. Since a person is raised in a sub-culture, his "self" develops as a function of that sub-culture. When he/she moves from it into the larger group, this self may no longer be consistent with the demand of the new group. His actions may continue to be appropriate to the perceptions of self he derived from the previous group and may appear to him to be completely adequate. To the larger society, his actions may appear to be unusual or even abnormal, depending on how far they deviate form the expectations of the large group.

Not only do culturally defined standards of social desirability govern the recognition of particular qualities in oneself, but also they provide the yardstick or standard against which one gauges his regard for himself. The position one occupies in the social class hierarchy of his society is related to his conception of himself and his self esteem. Individuals who rank higher on the social class ladder typically express greater self esteem and show less evidence of feelings of personal inadequacy than do individuals at the low end of the ladder. Similarly, members of minority groups typically show low levels of self-concept and evidence feelings of inferiority.

Physical body, a very primitive aspect of self-perception involves perception of the physical self, or body image. Phychologists describe, that, everything within the integumental limits of the self-concept, the perception of the physical self, not only constitutes the primitive core of the self-concept, even in maturity. This happens so, because others perceive and react to an individual at least particularly in terms of his size, skin colour, appearance, and the physical make-up. The individual's perception of himself reflects considerable attention to such features.

Gilmer (1970) argues that the most material and visible part of the self is the body. We look at our hands in relation to what they can do, at our eyes and mouth in terms of sense reception and behavioural expression, and some of us look at our skin in terms of the reaction it will evoke in others. Since one's body is an intimate thing and its perception becomes firmly established, it is very difficult to change such perception. The body is perceived through the senses. One explores his/her surroundings with sights, sounds and smells. The body of an individual occupies a central role in his/her perception as well as acts as an instrument of perception of self. The way one perceives his/her physical body may have psychological consequences for him/her.

Physical ability is the prerequisite by which the physically challenged children learn about themselves. Individuals whose bodies are impaired by disease, injury or deformity tend to suffer in developing self-concept. Body deformities and physical abnormalities seriously affect the self-perception of the physically challenged children. Because of functional limitation of body parts, the physically challenged children experience difficulties in learning about their world. Since the primary means of learning in the early years of life is acquired through actions, limited physical functioning can retard self-concept formation. Individuals with handicapping conditions experience greater difficulty in facing the socially accepted points of reference because they are different from the other non-physically challenged people. They find it difficult to grow up with the expectation based on what the average people are around them do and work to achieve. They have few norms to guide them and there is the possibility of an unclear and confused self-concept.

Individuals with handicapping conditions are generally brought up with unrealistic aspirations. They may think of becoming physicians, airplane pilots or mechanics which are unlikely to be feasible. When the physically challenged children enter into the school, they find themselves unsuitable for a number of activities. This develops a feeling of inadequacy, uncertainty, low self-esteem. Such psychological feelings further lead to poor adjustment and development of negative self-concept.

During adolescence, appearance of secondary sex characteristics and body image no doubt affect one's self-concept development. An existing defect and impaired physique during the adolescence stage become extremely frustrating and discouraging to the physically challenged individual's emotional stability. Such emotional tension which is painful and unpleasant becomes difficult to reduce. The superego experiences more punishment than reward and the physically challenged individuals feel uncertain, inadequate, inferior and socially unacceptable. Unfavourable experience in different crisis points signify a sense of failure and incompetence. That is why most of the physically challenged adolescents develop negative self-concept. This negative psychological impact leads the physically challenged individuals to perceive themselves as sick irrespective of their real self. Some disabled individuals expect others to perform roles appropriate to a sick person. This usually involves expecting to be looked after, and absolved of responsibility. Such overgeneralized sick self-perception conceals the physically challenged individual's real potential. In such cases there may be underestimation of oneself and the self-concept formed is not appropriate to the real self.

Social influence no doubt shows that self is a fragile concept largely dependent on the opinion of others. Physical limitation and the source constraints primary and secondary to the handicap do create a sick self-concept which is characterized by demanding and dependent character. However, not all individuals with handicapping conditions do possess low self-concept and play the "sick role". Some of them also have positive self-concept.

Bala (1985) reports that orthopaedically handicapped children appear to be reserved, stiff, detached, emotionally less stable, submissive, serious with superego, dependent, withdrawn, shy and apprehensive. Deaf children appear to be deliberate, inactive, phlegmatic, prudent and tender minded. Visually impaired children possess poor ideal, social and perceived self-concept.

According to Vespi and Yewchuk (1992), the talented/gifted handicapped individuals possess fragile self-concept. They struggle with self acceptance. They have feelings of social discomfort, and shame. They possess intense frustration and anger. They experience interpersonal difficulties with peers, teachers and family. These individuals always need sources to release pent-up energies.

Self-concept tends to stabilize with increasing age, but this is not a uniform growth process. Generally speaking, higher levels of self esteem accompany greater stability of self-concept.

Inappropriate development of self may be associated with dysfunctions of psychological adjustment. Failure to evolve a well integrated self esteem leads to a fragmented and disorganized self-concept. Even when the self-concept is reasonably orderly and coherent, one feels very disapproving about the content of the self-concept, reflecting low self-esteem. Low self esteem tends to make people set two goals for themselves, resulting in poor achievement motivation, lack of persistence and ambition, and even social withdrawal or isolation. Poor self-concept and low self-esteem often result from excessive failure and punishment and are associated with the exceptional children.

Learning Style—What it is? Various Types of Learning Styles

Learning style represents an important component of the learning process. The term "learning style" generally refers to a learner's characteristic approach to learning. The term has been used in the literature in two distinct ways:

1. It has been used to indicate a broad description or relatively consistent behaviours related to ways of going about learning, it is treated as an individual difference of generality comparable to intelligence or personality, but describing consistency in the ways people tackle learning tasks.
2. The definition has been narrowed considerably to parallel the idea of congnitive style, with the use of bipolar traits, but described in relation to the learning tasks commonly found in educational contexts, as opposed to scores on psychological tests. Both uses of the term imply that learning style is related both to cognitive process and personality. In both senses, the term has been used to cover a range of concepts which have emerged from attempts to describe aspects of student's learning.

Before making broad explanation of the term "learning style", let us cite some definitions given in psychology and education.

1. **Shearer and Tallmodge (1969):** In the views of Shearer and Tallmodge, learning style is an attribute of an individual which interacts with instructional circumstances in such a way as to produce differential learning achievement as a function of these circumstances.
2. **D.A. Kolb (1976):** According to Kolb, learning style is a result of heredity, experience and present environment and each one's learning style is a combination of four basic modes, namely, concrete experience, reflective observation, abstract conceptualization, and active experimentation.
3. **Claxton and Ralston (1978):** In the words of Claxton and Ralston, the term learning style refers to "a student's consistent way of responding to, and using, stimuli in the context of learning".
4. **Keefe (1979):** Keefe conceptualized learning styles as comprising of three types of behaviours; cognitive, affective and physiological/physical. A cognitive behaviour refers to a preference for a given type of information processing; an affective behaviour indicates the attitude or opinion of a learner; and physiological/physical behaviours are of two types; environmental factors that impinge on learning and biological factors in the make up of the individual that have an impact on the learning situation.

5. **Pask (1983):** Pask defines learning style as an individual's general tendency to adopt a particular strategy.

6. **Dunn, Dunn and Price (1985):** In the words of Dunn, Dunn and Price, learning style could be defined in terms of individual student reaction to various elements of instructional environments, immediate environment, emotionality, grouping preferences, psychological characteristics and physiological characteristics.

7. **Dececco and Crawford (1988):** In their views, learning styles are personal ways in which individuals process information in the course of learning new concepts and principles.

8. **Schmeck (1988):** Schmeck defines learning styles as the peculiar combination of strategies and processes a student habitually employs when trying to learn new material.

9. **Lynn Curry (1991):** In the views of Lynn Curry, learning style is the indvidual's intellectual approach to adopting and assimilating information.

In classifying the meaning of the term learning style it would be better to see it in relation to other terms like learning strategy, learning ability, cognitive style, and cognitive processes etc. The term *learning strategy* can be explained in terms of "a mechanism by which the individual copes up with the particular learning environment." An individual chooses a learning strategy whether or not a particular learning environment matches his or her learning style. The term *learning ability* refers to "an individual's potential performance given a defined setting and a defined task demand". The term *cognitive style* could be defined as "the individual's approach to adopting and assimilating information, but this adaptation does not interact directly with the environment; rather, this is an underlying and relatively permanent personality of level dimension that becomes manifest only indirectly and by looking for universals within an individual across many learning instances".

"Cognitive processes" are basic cognitive activities taking place within the memory, involving coding or thinking processes which are usually investigated within laboratory experiments. When these processes are described in terms of the ability of individual's consistently to carry out certain types of tasks such as certain

psychological tests, they are referred to as "cognitive skills". In everyday life, skills are brought into play in order to solve particular problems or to deal effectively with certain situations. Here a decision is required to select particular skills, or to apply processes in succession, within some overall plan. This can be seen as adopting "tactics". And if an organized series of tactics is required, perhaps depending also on a person's attitudes and motives then these may be called strategies. Finally if a person tends to adopt a similar set of strategies consistently across different tasks, this can be taken to indicate the existence of "learning styles".

The various types of learning styles are:

I. Learning Style Based on Cognitive Functioning

(a) Cognitive Learning Style

Research into cognitive learning styles has developed from attempts to predict different levels and types of academic performance in students. Some of the earliest attempts to describing different learning styles came from the attention given to divergent thinking by J.P. Guilford, Wallach and Kogan (1965), and Hudson (1966) drew attention to the existence of two distinct groups of children. Those with much higher scores on intelligence than creativity were labelled "convergers", while those with reverse pattern of scores were called divergers.

Kolb (1983) also used the terms convergers and divergers, but with a rather different meaning. In Kolb's views convergers prefer abstract material and process it actively, while the divergers look for concrete information and process it reflectively. Other than these two, Kolb also stated two other types of learning i.e., assimilators (abstractions processed reflectively) and accomodators (active, concrete). These are parallels here with C.G. Jung's "psychological types" and with the distinctive thinking processes attributed to extroverts and introverts.

(b) Information Processing Learning Style

Biggs (1987) has used ideas derived from information processing theories to investigate the ways in which students learn and study. His three categories of learning styles describe characteristically different strategies for dealing with information which are related to the intentions and underlying motives of the learner. The styles here are actually referred to as "approaches to learning" due to similarities which were demonstrated with the concept introduced by Marton (Marton, Hounsell, and Entwistle 1984). According to Biggs, a "deep" approach brings together intrinsic and competence motivation with a learning strategy which involves the attempt to understand the meaning of what is being learned. An "achieving" approach is rooted in competition and ego enhancement and leads to a strategy which depends on well organized study methods. Finally, a "surface" approach is driven by fear and leads to a dependency on reproduction through rote learning.

Although these three descriptions of learning styles do contain both cognitive components, the descriptions put more emphasis on their cognitive origins.

II. Bipolar Learning Styles

(a) Holist vs. Serialist Learning Style

Messick (1976) states that cognitive styles have most commonly been measured through perceptual tests such as the Embedded Figures Test or the Matching Familiar Figure Test. In contrast learning styles have been identified either by observing students working on learning tasks, or from inventory scores. Biggs (1987) states that students have relatively strong and consistent preferences for adopting a particular type of strategy, which he takes to indicate their learning style.

Some students adopt a "holist" style in which, right from the start, they try to see the task in widest possible perspective, establishing an overview which goes well beyond the task itself. Their learning process involves the use of illustrations, examples, analogies and anecdotes in building up an idiosyncratic form of understanding deeply rooted in personal experience and beliefs. Other students prefer a "serialist" style in which they begin with a narrow focus, concentrate on details and logical connections in a cautious manner, and look at the broader context only toward the end of the topic. Extreme holists are often impulsive, even cavalier, in their use of evidence, tending to generalize too readily and to jump to unjustified conclusions. Extreme serialists are often too cautious, failing to see important relationships or useful analogies, thus leaving their understanding improvised.

Pask follows Messick in arguing that learning styles are value differentiated. Students who have a strong preference for one or other style will find it difficult to shift strategy between different kinds of tasks. Pask showed that students learn more effectively from materials designed to match their particular learning style which reflects their own learning style. There thus seems to be considerable advantage in being able to adopt readily to different presentational styles, adopting what, Pask describes as "versatile" style. A student who is versatile is not prone to vacuous globetrotting; he does indeed build-up descriptions of what may be known by a rich use of analogical reasoning, but subjects the hypotheses to test and operationally verify the validity of an analogy and the limits of it's applicability. Pask's descriptions of styles of learning seem to overlap in places, with Marton's ideas about deep and surface approaches to learning.

(b) Learning style based on the functioning of "Left Cerebral Hemisphere" and "Right Cerebral Hemisphere"

Students who learn on the basis of the functioning of left cerebral hemisphere depend on verbal, analytic, abstract, temporal and digital operations and who learn on the basis of the functioning of right hemisphere are found to be non-verbal, holistic, concrete, spatial, analogical, creative, intuitive and aesthetic.

III. Learning Styles Based on "Conceptual Tempos" and "Selection Strategies"

(a) Conceptual Tempos

Conceptual tempos are basic dispositions of the individual either to reflect upon his solution of a problem or to make impulsive and unconsidered responses. According to Jerome Kagan and his associates (1964-1965, and 1966), the child with the impulsive, or fast tempo solves a problem with little or no delay, while the child with the reflective, or slow, tempo considers alternative problem solutions and, therefore, delays his responses.

(b) Selection Strategies

Jerome Bruner and his associates (1956) describe various ways in which individuals can learn concepts. These methods are called selection strategies. Four selection strategies have been identified. In the first of these, "conservative focusing", the individual uses an example of the concept as a focus and changes one attribute of the example at a time to find those attributes which are essential. In "focus gambling" strategy, the individual uses a focus example, but it is dissimilar to the previous one, here one changes more than one attribute at a time. In the two other selection strategies, "simultaneous scanning" and "successive scanning", the student formulates one or more hypotheses about the attributes. Individuals may vary their strategy with the concept or they may retain a particular strategy regardless the concept they seek to acquire.

On the basis of the above stated types of learning styles it could be said that an individual shows strong and relatively consistent preferences for tackling learning tasks in distinctive ways which vary from individual to individual.

Learning Styles—Theoretical Perspectives

Though work on learning style is of recent origin, several theories have been developed. Various theories on learning style could be clustered into three groups. One group of theoreticians, namely Friedman and Stritter, Rezler and Schmeck have laid emphasis on "instructional preference" in understanding learning style. Another group of theoreticians while explaining learning style have stressed on the individual's approach to adopting and assimilating information. Theoreticians, like Kolb, Tamir, Elstein, Molidor, Grasha and Richman could be included into this group. The third group of theoreticians like Witkin, Myers-Briggs and Kagan, while explaining the term learning style has given more emphasis on "cognitive style". They also define learning style as the individual's approach to adopting and assimilating information, but this adaptation does not interact with the environment, rather this is an underlying and relatively permanent dimension that becomes manifest only indirectly and by looking for universals within an individual across many learning instances. Theoreticians from time to time have attempted to study "learning styles" from cognitive and affective perspectives, while in few cases focus has been given on the perceptual modalities of the learner. Out of various theories, the theory of learning style which has received most attention in recent years is that of Kolb (1976, 1984). His theory popularly known as "experiential learning theory" has been widely accepted and put into researches across the world. In the present study the concept of learning style as postulated by Kolb (1976, 1984) in his "experiential learning theory" has been used. That is why in the present study, the researcher thought it wise to cite in detail the "experiential learning theory" of Kolb.

Experiential Learning Theory of Kolb (1976, 1984)

A pioneer in the development of learning style theory, David A. Kolb (1976) proposed a model which suggests that learning style is a result of heredity, experience and present environment. His typology included four phases of the learning cycle; concrete experience, Reflective observation, abstract conceptualization, and active experimentation. Based on his typology he developed his learning style inventory which compares favourably to many measures which assess various aspects of learning. Focusing on the polar extremes of the concrete—abstract and active—reflective dimensions of congnitive growth, he describes a four-stage cycle of learning. He argues that concrete experience (CE) leads to reflective observation (RO) followed by the development of abstract conceptualization (AC). This piece of knowledge is then tested by active experimentation (AE), which itself produces new concrete experiences so that the cycle is completed and begins anew. Kolb's four phases of the learning cycle—concrete experience, reflective observation, abstract conceptualization and active experimentation has been shown in the diagram (see page 39).

According to Kolb, effective learners rely on four different learning modes: concrete experience, reflective observation, abstract conceptualization and active experimentation. That is they must be able to involve themselves fully, openly, and without bias in

KOLB'S LEARNING CYCLE BY—D.A. KOLB (1984)

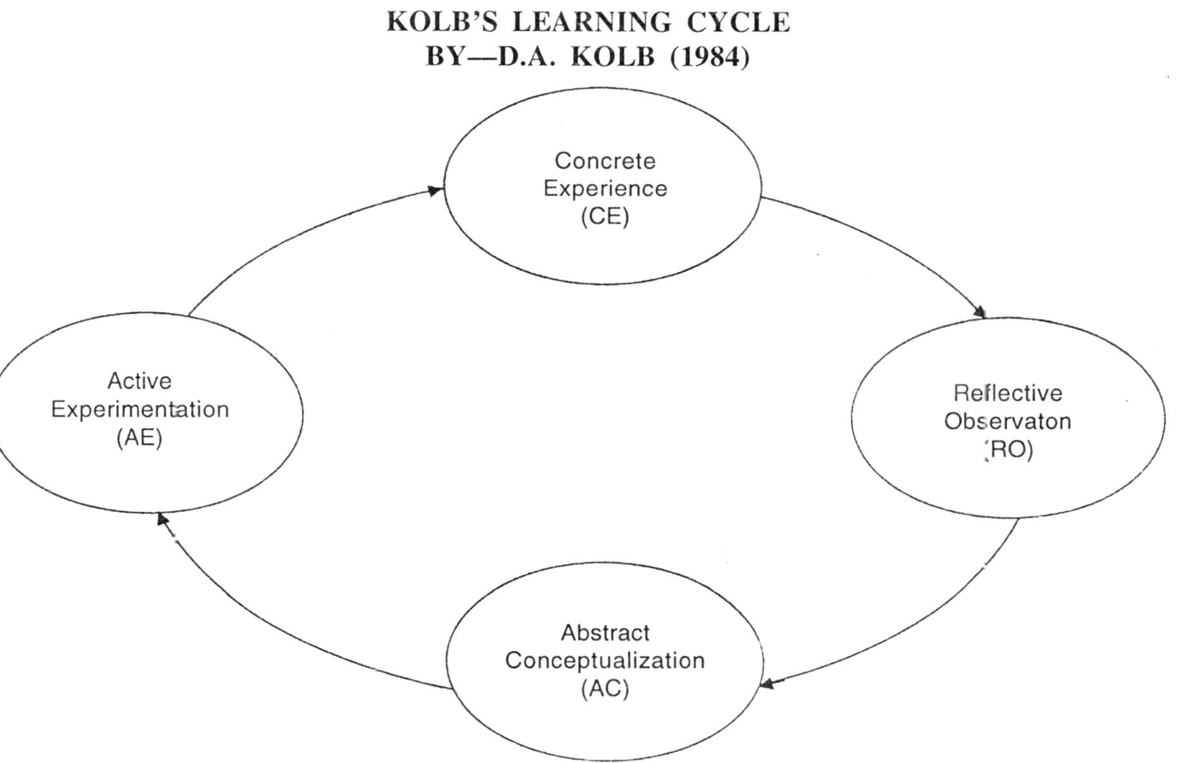

new experiences (CE), they must be able to reflect on and observe these experiences from many perspectives (RO); they must be able to create concepts that integrate their observations into logically sound theories (AC); and they must be able to use these theories to make decisions and solve problems (AE).

There are several observations to be made about the model shown by Kolb. First the learning cycle is continuously recurring. It implies that an individual tests his/her concepts in experience and modifies them as a result of own observation of the experience.

Second, the direction that learning takes place is governed by one's felt needs and goals. An individual seeks experiences that are related to his/her goals, interpret them in the light of his/her goals, and form concepts and test implications of these concepts that are relevant to those felt needs and goals.

Third, since learning process is directed by individual needs and goals, learning styles become highly individual in both direction and process. For example, a mathematician may come to place great emphasis on abstract concepts, whereas a poet may value concrete experience more highly. A manager may be primarily concerned with active application of concepts, whereas a naturalist may develop observational skills highly. This shows that each individual in a more personal way develops a learning style. One may jump into experiences but fails to observe the lessons to be derived from these experiences; one may form concepts but fails to test their validity.

While describing learner's characteristics with regard to one's preferred learning style, Kolb explains that an orientation toward concrete experience focuses on being involved in experiences and dealing with immediate human situations in a personal way. It emphasizes feeling as opposed to thinking, a concern with the uniqueness and complexity of present reality as opposed to theories and generalizations, an intuitive, "artistic" approach as opposed to the systematic, scientific approach to problems. People with a concrete experience orientation enjoy and are good at relating to others. They are often good intuitive decision makers and function well in unstructured situations. People with this orientation value relating to people, being involved in real situations, and an open minded approach to life.

An orientation toward reflective observation focuses on understanding the meaning of ideas and situations by carefully observing and impartially describing them. It emphasizes understanding as opposed to practical application, a concern with what is true or how things happen as opposed to what is practical, an emphasis on reflection as opposed to action. People with a reflective orientation enjoy thinking about the meaning of situations and ideas and are good at seeing their implications. They are good at looking at things from different perspectives and at appreciating different points of view. They like to rely on their own thoughts and feelings to form opinions. People with this orientation value patience, impartiality, and considered thoughtful judgement.

An orientation toward abstract conceptualization focuses on using logic, ideas, and concepts. It emphasizes thinking as opposed to feeling, a concern with building general theories as opposed to intuitively understanding unique, specific areas, a scientific, as opposed to an artistic, approach to problems. A person with an abstract conceptual orientation enjoys and is good at systematic planning, manipulation of abstract symbols, and quantitative analysis. People with this orientation value precision, the rigour and discipline of analyzing ideas, and the aesthetic quality of a neat conceptual system.

An orientation toward "active experimentation" focuses on actively influencing people and changing situations. It emphasizes practical applications as opposed to reflective understanding, a pragmatic concern with what works as opposed to what is absolute truth, an emphasis on doing as opposed to observing. People with an active experimentation orientation enjoy and are good at getting things accomplished. They are willing to take some risk to achieve their objectives. They also value having an impact and influence on the environment around them and like to see results.

Elements that Affect Learning Styles

Elements that affect learning styles are:

A. Environmental Elements

B. Psychological Elements

C. Sociological Elements

D. Physical Elements.

A. Environmental Elements

(a) **Sound:** Sound is an important factor that affects child's way of learning. Some children can work easily with noise by ignoring or blocking them out. While some need a relatively quiet environment, and others require silence before they can concentrate. Knowing this, one can understand how necessary it is to design an instructional environment that includes areas and sections where students that need to may talk, interact, and share and areas, where others may work alone in quiet.

(b) **Light:** Light is a factor that appears to affect fewer people than does sound. Although some students are light sensitive and can tolerate only subdued lighting and others are light needy and require extremely bright lights before they can engage in reading or writing activities comfortably, most seem to be relatively unaffected by normal variations of light.

(c) **Temperature:** Individual reactions to temperature are unique. Some students can concentrate better when the environment is cool; when it becomes warm they feel drowsy and cannot function well. Others cannot concentrate when they are cool; anything other than warmth can cause physical or emotional discomfort and can affect their mode of learning.

B. Psychological Elements

(a) **Motivation:** Motivation plays a crucial role in making a child to learn. A motivated learner seems to be eager to learn while an unmotivated learner needs various modes and complements to learn a task.

(b) **Persistence:** Persistence could be better explained in terms of span of attention. Students vary with regard to their span of attention. Those who have good span of attention work on a task until it is completed. In contrast students with short attention span cannot continue their work for any length of time. Such children lose interest, become irritated, begin to daydream, or become involved in social activities rather than completing their task or learning a study material.

(c) **Responsibility:** Invariably students are found both responsible and irresponsible. Those who are responsible follow through on a given task, complete it to the best of their ability. Those who are not responsible, when they find a task difficult for them, rather than seeking help they permit their attention to be diverted and become troublesome and cause a general disturbance.

(d) **Structure:** Structure is the establishment of specific rules for working on and completing an assignment. It implies that certain things should be completed in a specific way within a definite time span. Structure limits the number of options that are available to a student and requires an imposed mode of either learning, responding, or demonstrating achievement. Motivated, persistent, responsible students usually require little structure and supervision, certainly for less than do the unmotivated—those who are not persistent and responsible.

(e) **Sociological Elements:** Students learn in a variety of sociological patterns that include working alone, with one or two friends, with a small group or as a part of a team, with adults, or, for some, in any variation thereof. It is important to identify how each student learns and to then assign to that individual the correct grouping, methods and resources.

D. Physical Elements

(a) **Perceptual Strength:** Students vary in their perceptual modalities so far as their learning is concerned. The various modalities students adopt are auditory, visual, tactual and kinesthetic. Those who learn through auditory sense can differentiate among sounds and can produce symbols, letters or words by hearing them. Those who learn through their visual sense can associate shapes and words and conjure up the image of a form by seeing in their mind. Students learning through tactual sense cannot begin to associate word formations and meanings without involving in a sense of touch. Students learning through their kinesthetic sense need to have real life experiences in order to learn to recognize words and their meanings. However there are also students who need a combination of multi-sensory resources. Many of the children with handicapping conditions adopt any one or many modalities, which could be termed as their learning styles.

(b) **Time:** The proverbial night owls and eager beavers are dramatically opposite in their learning styles. One comes alive late at night and the other functions at maximum capacity early in the morning. Some students can perform well at one time of day, and others achieve most effectively at the opposite time. This states that time appears to be an important factor that affects one's learning style.

(c) **Mobility:** Some students need a great deal of mobility in the learning environment and cannot function well unless permitted to vary their position and location often while others are able to complete a task while in one physical position for a comparatively long period of time. The desire for mobility is a conglomerate function of one's physical, emotional, and environmental reactions, but most students cannot easily control their need to move while learning. However, mobility is found to be an important factor in affecting one's learning styles.

Understanding Motivation

The term motivation has been derived from the Latin word *"movere"*, means *"to move"*. The term has been used with different connotations in the past, sometimes interchangeably with terms like internal urge, aspiration, need, motive, drive, desire etc. The term instinct is used generally with reference to animal behaviour, drive in relation to infra-human behaviour, and motive or need in the context of human behaviour.

The meaning of motivation had been a controversial issue in the field of psychology. At one time, motivation was the dominant field of study and was conceived as "what moves a resting organism to a state of activity". A shift from "behavioural field" to "cognitive perspective" in psychology, brought change in the concept of motivation.

For Jones (1955) the term motivation comprises answers to such questions as how behaviour gets started, is energized, is sustained, is stopped and what kind of subjective reaction is present in the organism while all this is going on.

Atkinson (1964) defines motivation as contemporary (immediate) influence on the direction, vigour, and persistence of action.

For Berelson and Steiner (1964) a motive is an inner urge, that energizes, activates or moves (hence motivation) and that directs or chanellizes towards goals.

In the views of Gellerman (1968), to steer one's actions towards certain goals and to commit a certain part of one's energies to reaching them is motivation.

Vernon (1969) defines motivation as a kind of force which arouses, regulates and sustains all our more important actions.

Sarford and Wrightman (1970) define motivation in terms of motive. To them motive is restlessness, a lack, a yearn, a force. Once in the grip of motive, the organism does something to reduce the restlessness, to remedy the lack to alleviate the yearn, to mitigate the force.

Logan and Ferraro (1978) define motivation as a hypothetical state resulting from deprivation or stimulation and reflected in a relatively transitory effect on performance.

The above stated definitions attempt to focus on three major components of motivation which are:

(a) the force or capacity that energizes behaviour,

(b) directionality of behaviour, i.e., effort being expanded in particular direction to achieve a particular goal or objective; and

(c) persistence of directional behaviour till the goal or objective by the yearn or lack, and emotional reactions in case of goal not being achieved.

In behavioural language, motivation has been explained in terms of descriptions of the direction, vigour, and persistence of observable environmental conditions. The primary interest in the study of motivation is to identify and to understand the effects of all the important contemporaneous influences which determine the direction of action, its vigour and its persistence.

Common sense regards a "motive" as the factor that explains the direction, vigour, and persistence of an individual's actions. A motive, as defined by habitual usage, is something (as a need or desire) that causes a person to act. The origin of our impulses to do this or that whether called a want, a wish, or desire are all the more generally considered motives which make an individual into action.

Theories of Motivation

Over the last few decades, theoreticians have attempted to develop theories to study motivational characteristics of an individual. Without going into the details of different theories and distinctions among them, a brief account is given here. Theories of motivation have broadly been classified into two groups, namely, (i) process theories and (ii) content theories.

(i) **Process theories** define the major variables which are necessary for explaining choice, effort and persistence. Incentive, drive, reinforcement and expectancy are major variables appearing in various models based on process theories. Such theories attempt to specify how the major variables interact to influence particular dependent variables. Drive theory (Hull, 1937), reinforcement theory (Skinner, 1948), expectancy-valence (Vroom, 1964) and equity theory (Adams, 1963) etc. are all process theories.

(ii) **Content theories** are more concerned with trying to specify the substantive identity of the variables that influence behaviour and less so with the process by which they do it. That is, what are the specific rewards people want? What are the basic needs which they try to satisfy? What incentives are most powerful? A content theory tries to identify the specific entities within a more general class. Need-press theory (Murray,

1938), Need hierarchy theory (Maslow, 1954), Two factor theory (Herzberg, Mausner, and Snynderman, 1959), E.R.G. (Existence, relatedness, and growth) model (Alderfer, 1969), Achievement motivation theory (Atkinson, Mc-Clelland, 1964) are all content theories.

Most content theories attempt to explain why does a person choose a particular action over the many alternatives that are available to him. Why do people continue a given action, even though other courses which might even be easier are open to them? While answering these questions of direction and persistence of action the use of concepts like wants or needs becomes imperative, for needs are considered to be initiating and sustaining forces of behaviour. They have a direct influence on an individual since they determine in part his/her thoughts and actions. A person's needs working in conjunction with his/her emotions and other psychological functions act as motives that dictate one's behaviour. An individual's perception of the real world about him/her, one's feelings and current activities—all these processes and many more are influenced by his/her needs.

The concept of human needs is relevant to one's behaviour. Some psychologists have postulated only one basic need (Goldstein, 1947, Rogers, 1963), some have postulated three basic needs Mc-Clelland, 1951, Alderfer, 1969), some postulated five basic needs (Maslow, 1943), whereas others have listed hundreds of needs. (e.g. Murray, 1938). Such varied listing indicates that the number of needs postulated has depended rather on the degree of specificity with which one chooses to analyse them. Maslow (1943) states that in human life there exists a hierarchy of needs. Growth is achieved by progressively satisfying the needs starting from the basic needs to the other higher order needs like self actualization. These needs and corresponding goals are inherent in human nature but the realization of a higher need is only possible when the lower needs have been satisfied.

With researchers now concentrating on human behaviour, motivational research seems to be dominated by investigations into human's need for achievement (Weiner, 1990). Also called incentive motivation, effectance, and the urge for mastery, achievement motivation is thought to be a fundamental tendency of humans to manipulate, dominate, or otherwise master their environment. Among the most prominent researchers in achievement motivation were David Mc-Clelland, and John Atkinson. They sought to understand why some people appear to strive for excellence simply for the sake of achieving while others don't. Mc-Clelland, Atkinson, Clark and Lowell, 1953). The theory of achievement motivation as postulated by Mc-Clelland and Atkinson has and had a significant role in the literature of motivation. This theory appears to be important if we are to study the motivational behaviour of an individual.

Achievement Motivation—A Theoretical Perspective

The theory of achievement motivation attempts to account for the determinants of the direction, magnitude, and persistence of behaviour in a limited but very important domain of human activities. It applies only when an individual knows that his/her performance will be evaluated (by himself or by others) in terms of some standard of excellence and that the consequence of his/her actions will be either a favourable evaluation (success) or an unfavourable evaluation (failure). It is, in the other words, a theory of achievement-oriented performance. In the views of Mc-Clelland, the disposition called achievement motive might be conceived as a capacity for taking pride in accomplishment when success at one or another activity is achieved. Obviously, if success and failure are alternative outcomes when performance is evaluated in relation to some criterion of skill, the expectancy of failure must be weak when expectancy of success is strong and vice-versa.

It is assumed that a high need for achievement develops in children whose parents stress achievement and competitiveness at home. But achievement motivation can also be situationally affected. Individuals would work harder under certain conditions, such as particular test instructions, competitive environments, and failure (Atkinson, 1964). Atkinson's findings have been paralleled by investigations into other individual variables related to motivation. Besides having high or low achievement motivation, people can have high or low anxiety (Spielberger, 1966), or high or low internal control (Rottor, 1966). Excessive anxiety can interfere with learning and performance, leading to a reduction in continuing motivation to learn. Conversely, students show greater motivation when they have an internal, as opposed to external, orientation. This means they tend to perceive learning tasks as skill determined and thus subject to personal control. Externally oriented students tend to believe that their success at a learning task will be determined by chance rather than by means within their control. These students are therefore less likely to be motivated to engage in the learning task.

Atkinson (1964) further states that the motive to achieve success, which the individual carries about with him from one situation to another, combines multiplicatively with the two specific situational influences, the strength of expectancy or probability of success (Ps) and incentive value of success at a particular activity (Is) to produce the tendency to approach success that is overtly expressed in the direction, magnitude and persistence of achievement-oriented performance. In other words, the strength of motivation to achieve, or tendency to approach success (Ts) through performance of certain actions, may be represented as:

$$\mathbf{Ts = Ms \times Ps \times Is}$$

[Strength of motivation to achieve = Motive to achieve success x probability of success x incentive value of success]

The first variable (Ms), is a relatively general and stable characteristic of the person which is present in any behaviour situation. But the values of the other two variables Ps and Is depend upon the individual's past experience in specific situations that are similar to one he/she now confronts. These variables change as the individual moves about from one life situation to another and so are treated as characteristics of particular situations or particular tasks.

In addition to a general disposition to seek success called the achievement motive there is also a general disposition to avoid failure called motive to avoid failure. Where the motive to achieve could be characterized as a capacity for reacting with pride in accomplishment, the motive to avoid failure can be conceived as a capacity for reacting with same when the outcome performance is failure. Such a motivation generally arouses with an individual when it is clear that performance will be evaluated and failure is a distinct possibility. In such case, anxiety and a tendency to withdraw from the situation take place.

The potentiality or ability of a child seems to have influences on his/her motivational disposition in academic situation. Research studies depict that children with high achievement motivation tend to prefer tasks which require initiative, inventiveness and which present some intellectual difficulty, a challenge to their success. Such children generally are found to be risk taking individuals. Those with moderate achievement motivation might become anxious over probability of failure when achievement is demanded and they perform less well. Those with strong achievement motivation are not frustrated with failure in a task because it helps them to determine more firmly to achieve a goal they set for themselves. Children with high anxiety and low achievement motivation prefer to have task at a very easy level where they are unlikely to fail. Children with strong achievement motivation generally do well in school, are self-reliant and less dependent on others. Mc-Clelland (1961) showed that achievement motivation is a fairly stable characteristic and is correlated with actual achievement in real-life situations.

Relationship Between Motivation and Learning Styles

Motivation can be seen to influence not just the degree of effort one puts into school work, but also the type of efforts and style of learning one adopts. Entwistle (1983) reports that the three forms of motivations, namely, intrinsic motivation, fear of failure motivation, and need for achievement (n-ach) do definitely influence one's learning style. The three styles of learning for which Entwistle advocates are deep approach, surface approach and strategic approach. Intrinsic motivation is always closely related to deep approach, "fear of failure" motivation is associated with surface approach, and need for achievement motivation is associated with strategic approach of learning.

Students with intrinsic motivation and adopting deep approach of learning do possess intention to understand a task, want to have vigorous interaction with content, relate the new ideas to previous knowledge, relate concepts to everyday experience, and learn with a purpose to examine the logic of the argument that leads to draw conclusions.

Students displaying fear of failure motivation and adopting surface approach learning style do only possess an intention to complete task requirements. They memorize informations needed for assessments and treat task as an external imposition. They learn by focusing on discrete elements without integration of a task. They do not possess ability to distinguish principles from examples.

Students possessing "need for achievement" motivation and adopting "strategic approach" as their preferred learning style do use well planned and carefully organized study methods. They do depend on a systematic management of time and effort geared to the perceived demands of the assessment procedures. They do have the intention to highest possible grades for which they ensure conditions and study materials for studying appropriate.

Like "motivation", "interest" and "anxiety" of an individual also affect his/her style of learning. It has been found out (Fransson, 1987) that students who find study material or a piece of learning task interesting do adopt "deep approach" as their preferred learning style. While students when find a study task anxiety provoking tend to rely on "surface approach" to be their style of learning.

The above stated findings state that motivation of an individual affects his/her learning style. To support Entwistle, findings of Schmeck (1988) could be cited here. Schmeck (1988) related his studies of learning styles with personality (self) aspect of an individual. According to Schmeck, the introvert is seen as adopting a deep style which develops effective schema and conceptions through articulated or field independent thinking processes involving predominantly analytic and synthetic reasoning. The stable extrovert is more likely to use an elaborative style which involves an impulsive personalizing of knowledge through global or field dependent thinking, making substantial use of examples and concrete instances, often drawn from real world experiences. Finally, the anxious individual is likely to be categorized as having a shallow style which depends on memorizing, or repetitive rehearsal of information leading to the literal reproduction of what was studied.

There remains considerable debate about the nature, and even the existence of learning styles. There is, however, substantial evidence to note that people do show strong and relatively consistent preferences for tackling learning tasks in distinctive ways.

Learning Styles and Motivational Characteristics of the Talented Exceptional Children

Orthopaedically impaired, visually impaired and speech and hearing impaired children vary among themselves so far as their learning styles and motivational characteristics are concerned. The functional limitations endowed on the physically challenged children make them different from the general run of population. Many of them learn verbally, some visually, some physically and kinesthetically and some through sign languages.

Orthopaedically impaired children vary widely in the nature and severity of their conditions. Many of them learn with ordinary teaching methods while others require special methods. Many students fall behind their age mates in academic achievements even though they have normal intelligence and motivation. Some children with mild or transitory physical problems have no academic deficiencies at all, others have severe difficulties. Some students who have serious health problems also manage to achieve at a high level and possess high intellectual ability with high motivation.

For the visually impaired children lack of vision causes a detachment from the physical and to some extent from the social environment. A visually impaired child cannot inform himself at a glance of his situation within a given environment as a sighted person can do. Because they lack one source of sensory input, their perceptual processes are different. They don't grasp many of the learning tasks and need more experiences than the sighted children. Abstractions such as the concept of colour may never be formed, since the child has no possibility of acquiring a background of sensory input for this concept. Learning of such concepts for them take place through vicarious experiences. In this area, the child experiences difficulty. Similarly learning of concept related to time and distance also take place through kinesthetic experiences. Thus, the visually impaired children are poor in abstract conceptualization and in learning by doing. They mostly rely on tactual and kinesthetic experiences for learning various tasks. Despite the fact that the visually impaired children lack vision, many of them possess high achievement motivation.

For the speech and hearing impaired children, lack of ability to listen and communicate contributes for poor language development. Learning of various tasks takes place through sign languages and reflective observations. Their learning of new objects seems to be based on the perceptual features like shape, colour, size texture and taste of things.

Pledgie (1982) while quoting the learning and motivational characteristics of the gifted/talented physically challenged children reports that these children have advanced, expressive and elaborate vocabulary. They memorize and recall information quickly and are aware of cause and effect relationships and can question and apply information. They are good in divergent thinking. They can generalize and provide more than one correct answer. They possess a prolonged attention span. They are curious to explore the environment. They possess a variety of interests. They display risk taking behaviour and possess a good sense of humour. Such children possess high achievement motivation and are advanced in many of the academic endeavours.

Conclusion

The theoretical backdrop of the study highlights concepts and theories on self, learning styles and motivational characteristics with special reference to the talented exceptional children. To understand perception of self, learning styles and motivational characteristics of the talented exceptional children, it is important to comprehend:

1. The talented exceptional children constitute unique and in some way a separate group. These children cannot be studied in terms of those principles of learning, thinking, perceiving and adjusting which have been derived from, and applicable to, normal ones.
2. Development of self follows the same course that occurs with the development of other kinds of cognitive concepts. Among the many forces that contribute for the development of self are language, personal success and failure, social interaction and physical body.

3. Physical ability is the prerequisite by which the physically challenged children learn about themselves. Body deformities and physical abnormalities seriously affect the self-perceptions of the physically challenged children. The talented exceptional children possess a fragile self-concept and struggle with self acceptance.
4. Learning style generally reflects a learner's characteristic approach to learning. Out of various types of learning styles, Kolb's (1976) typology has got wide acceptance. It emphasizes on four learning styles, namely, concrete experience, abstract conceptualization, reflective observation and active experimentation. Literature supports that learning style has substantial relationship with self-concept and is affected by one's motivational characteristics. Talented exceptional children vary among themselves while choosing their learning styles.
5. Achievement motivation is thought to be a fundamental tendency of an individual to manipulate, dominate or otherwise master his/her environment. It attempts to account for the determinants of the direction, magnitude, and persistence of behaviour of an individual in different activities. A motive to achieve arises in situations that offer the possibility of pride in accomplishment. It is assumed that "self-concept" is a relevant factor that interacts with motives in determining performance in achievement situations. Generally the exceptional children are reported to possess low achievement motivation.

After comprehending the theoretical backdrop, it is important to review the findings of researches who have dealt with the talented exceptional children in relation to their perception of self, learning styles and motivational characteristics.

3

Research Literature—A Critical Review

The review of literature involves locating, reading and evaluating reports of researches, observations and opinions that are related to the researcher's own study.

The review of related literature in educational research provides the researcher with the means of getting to the frontier in a particular field of knowledge. In any research work it is very much needed to know about what others have done and what remains to be explored that would contribute to develop knowledge in the field.

This chapter is divided into two sections. The first section encompasses the study findings conducted abroad, while the second section highlights the Indian studies. Presentation of review of related literature has been done chronologically.

Studies Conducted Abroad

Physically challenged children with potential gift or talent are identified for their handicap, not for their gifts or talents. Identifying the true ability of a physically challenged child and developing programmes accordingly presents a unique problem and a challenge to the researchers. The talented exceptional children constitute a very special, unique and different sub-population.

Most of the research studies conducted on the talented exceptional children have been done abroad. Many of these research findings are presented below in three subsections.

(*a*) Studies relating to various issues, identification and programming of the talented exceptional children.

(*b*) Studies relating to concept of self of the talented exceptional children.

(*c*) Studies relating to learning styles and motivational characteristics of the talented exceptional children.

Studies Relating to Various Issues, Identification and Programming of the Talented Exceptional Children

Our educational system is still lagging behind in developing appropriate procedures for identifying and programming for the gifted and/or talented children with handicapping conditions though the fact that these children would possess potential gift/talent is not a new one. Compared to the gifted/talented children in general these children do not get adequate professional support.

There have been little researches conducted with regard to identification and to know about the effectiveness of various programmes conducted on this sub-population of children. The few reports that exist depicting the status of these children are presented below:

Meisgeier, Charles; Neisgeir, Constance and Werblo, Dorothy (1978) stated that programs for the gifted handicapped are virtually non-existent. Educational personnel often place them in programs for the handicapped, which are often designed only to remediate the weak areas and offer little or no stimulus in the area of giftedness. More careful evaluation of handicapped students suspected of being gifted is needed and individualised programs should foster full development of their potential. Each child's school programme must be responsive to child's strengths and weaknesses.

Whitmore, J. R. (1981) argued that focus in educating gifted and talented handicapped children has been a problem. These children often had an opportunity to demonstrate their gifts. Accurate means of identifying and developing giftedness must be employed as well as strategies for overcoming handicaps in order to allow gifted handicapped individuals to realise their full potential.

Yarborough, Betty. H. and Johnson, Roger. A. (1983) conducted a survey of prevailing trends in gifted/talented identification procedures. Results reveal a theory-practice gap in gifted/talented programs. The most popular behavioural procedure used for identification was the demonstration of talent.

Karnes, M. B. (1984) discussed the "Retrieval and Acceleration of Promising Young Handicapped" (RAPYHT) project. Talent identification in this project involves the use of parent checklist and teacher checklist. Both instruments focused on children's performance in six areas of giftedness: intellectual, academic, creativity, leadership, visual and performing arts and psychomotor abilities.

Kegley, Sandra (1984) suggested that some universal considerations be included in every program for the gifted that are built upon the learning characteristic, styles and special needs of these students. Kegley's approach isolates responsibility, acceptance and love of learning as necessary components.

Betts, George T. (1986) described an approach to meeting the emotional and social needs of gifted individuals that includes seven separate categories of curriculum development contended to be necessary for their personal growth. Categories include the awareness, understanding and acceptance of self and others: interpersonal skills, group process and interaction skills, creativity, relaxation and visual imagery and support related to problems of being gifted.

Corn, Anne. L. (1986) while examining issues involving in educating visually handicapped gifted children, argued that it is critical for special educators to distinguish between normally functioning and gifted visually handicapped students. Obstacles with regard to identification include stereotype expectations, developmental delays, incomplete information, and lack of opportunity to superior mental abilities. He stresses more importance on self-system, and the need to look at disability, specific skills development for the purposes of the visually handicapped gifted children.

Felder, Richard, M. (1986) while focusing on identifying and dealing with exceptionally gifted children argued that I.Q. testing is an invaluable and irreplaceable tool for identifying gifted children and for obtaining a measure of their special educational needs. Felder suggests that early recognition and nurturance of giftedness lead to emotional well-being and to the development of self worth that provides the foundation for intellectual and moral development.

Feldusen, John. F. and Hoover, Steven. M. (1986) while reviewing current conceptions of giftedness and intelligence presented a conception of giftedness as an interaction of intelligence, special abilities or talents, self-concept, and resultant motivation to achieve. They also argue that motivation, self-concept and creativity should not serve as components of an identification scheme, but should be major goals of programs for the gifted.

Hemmings, Brain (1986) reported that as per research evidence, it could be suggested that identification, diagnosis and placement of children with potential gift and talent need to be done as early as possible to reduce problems such as under-achievement or poor motivation. A multidisciplinary approach that emphasises the significant roles played by teachers and parents of the gifted handicapped is necessary to identify, diagnose, and plan appropriately for their special educational needs. Programs should include the co-operative efforts of several disciplines including the medical, paramedical, counselling and guidance and social work professionals.

Hoge, Robert D. and Cudmore, Lausinde (1986) while reviewing the use of teacher judgement measures as a selection tool for identifying academically gifted pupils state that there is little basis for the negative assessment associated with these measures.

Karnes, Merle, B. and Johnson, Lowrence. J. (1986) argued for the early identification and programming for the young gifted/talented handicapped children. In their approach they laid stress on factors associated with the development of a retrieval and acceleration of promising young handicapped and talent programs were examined to illustrate the conceptualisation, dissemination and evaluation process in relation to the program's model for identifying and programming for young gifted/talented handicapped children. The goal of this program is to help handicapped children realise their potential through a focus on strengths and talents.

Sawyer, Robert N. (1986) stated the objectives of a talent identification program at an early age as to assist in the planning and implementation of programs to challenge these students, nurturing their talent through the critical middle and high school years, and assisting in their placement. It is argued that programs could be found effective in providing an opportunity for students to learn at their own pace and high level of comprehension, encouraging the development of support and coping strategies, and inspiring home and schools to provide more appropriate educational planning for the gifted. It is suggested that a parent may be the available significant person to appreciate the child's intense experience of meaning, joy, isolation, suffering, disappointment and awareness of the exquisite details in life. It also emphasised that the major problems and needs of the physically disabled individuals are physiological and psychological along with social. Problems of self-concept, body image, frustration, anger, dependency, and motivation are of special importance.

Wallace, Staurt D. (1986), while stressing on an approach towards meeting the needs of talented and exceptional pupils, advocated that the development of curriculum extension programs, set within the existing human and material resources of each school, are to be made to meet the immediate and specific needs and interests of pupils.

Whitmore, Joanne (1987) on topic conceptualising the issue of underserved population of gifted students, suggested that there are many subgroups of gifted students currently receiving no services or very limited special services, including those who lack general achievement motivation, those who experienced early difficulty in acquisition of basic skills, those who lack environmental nurturance of their potential, those with developmental delays, or those with specific learning disabilities. He points to the strong linkage between special education and gifted education and suggests that a stronger bond is needed among educators who teach children with special needs whatever those needs may be.

Barton, Jean M. and Starnes, Waveline T. (1989) investigated to identify distinguishing characteristics of gifted and talented learning-disabled students. Statistical analysis reflects commonalities with the general gifted population, and discriminant analysis showed patterns in achievement scores that may serve as markers to target those identified for in-depth evaluation for early identification. However, case cluster analysis showed that gifted talented learning-disabled population to be heterogeneous, suggesting that a single distinctive pattern is unlikely.

Culross, Rita (1989) discussed two issues inherent in current methods of identifying gifted students, i.e., the referral process and establishing standards for selection. Within the establishment of selection standards are issues of criteria, characteristics of educational setting, children's level of functioning, bias in the selection process, qualities of selection measures used, and the use of data derived from such measures. Rita argues that continuity of services based on broadly accepted definitions of giftedness should be a major goal of identification of the gifted.

Yewchuk, Carolyn R. and Bibby, Marry A. (1989a) described that gifted handicapped are often identified by their handicaps. Special training on needs and characteristics of gifted children and on appropriate teaching methods enable teachers of the handicapped to identify and adopt programs for the gifted handicapped children. Obstacles to identifying gifted handicapped learners include stereotypic expectations, handicapping effects and program limitations. Appropriate education programs for gifted handicapped children combine education principles from both handicapped and gifted programs, including development of self-concept, accurate diagnosis of strengths and weaknesses, teaching to strength and remediation of deficits.

Yewchuk, Carolyn R. and Bibby, Mary A. (1989b) conducted a study on identification of giftedness in severely and profoundly hearing impaired students by using non-verbal measures of I.Q., teacher nominations and parent nominations. No significant relationships emerged between parent nominations and I.Q. Although tending to nominate the same students, both teachers and parents missed identifying some gifted students. In the analysis of teacher nominations and I.Q., some significant relationships appeared for the public school students but not for the school for the deaf students. Teachers associated giftedness with the characteristics of superior recall, speed of understanding, reasoning ability, academic ability, expressive ability, eagerness to learn and keen observation.

Maxson, B.J., Tedder, Norma E., Marmion, Shelly and Lamb, Ann M. (1993) conducted a survey on 124 teachers of deaf blind students concerning their assessment of students and preferred teaching methods for five skill areas. The study indicated that teachers were goal directed, used flexibility and usually modified their instructions for usual students. However, the techniques that the teacher used most often appear to be at variance with the findings of studies on the learning needs of these students. That is, the teachers preferred methods of structuring learning tasks over methods stressing sensory input.

Vulliamy, Graham and Webb, Rosemary (1993) argued to use small N-studies within a positive framework. They also advocated for the use of qualitative research strategies, and the use of critical perspectives of sociologists. It is also argued that such developments have been largely restricted to disciplinary research, neglecting the 'pedagogic research' because special educational needs research has been dominated by those trained in psychology.

Blough, Lisa K., Ritten House, Robert K. and Daner, Jess (1999) compared teachers ratings of deaf students as gifted with scores of the Advanced Progressive Matrices (J. C. Raven, 1965) (APM) eleven deaf junior high school students were each classified as gifted and non-gifted by three school teachers. Results showed that teacher's rankings did not correlate with APM scores. No significant difference was found between mean raw scores on the APM of those classified as gifted vs. non-gifted. It is concluded that APM scores and teacher's rankings measure different things.

Summary of review of the above said sub-section

1. The orthopaedically impaired, speech and hearing impaired and visually impaired children with potential gift and or talent are underserved. Professional interest on these children is yet to get momentum.

2. Of all the sub-categories of talented/gifted children with handicapping conditions, the gifted learning-disabled children have received the most attention.
3. Identification of this sub-population of children tend to be difficult. Standardised psychological tools for the purpose of identification of talent of these children are of little use because most of the tools are standardised on normal children.
4. Teachers of the disabled children are less experienced with regard to the procedure involved in identifying the potential gift/talent of these children.
5. Educational programs for this sub-population of talented children are lacking and their problems are compounded by sometimes severe social problems and rock bottom feelings of self worth and personal integrity.

Studies Relating to Concept of Self of the Talented Exceptional Children

Handicapping conditions may cause developmental delays. **Maker (1977)** stated that cognitive development and intellectual functioning are delayed when certain handicapping conditions prevent or limit the child's ability to respond to cognitive stimulation and to demonstrate cognitive abilities through expression and problem solving.

Developmental delays also affect one's "self-concept development." Children with handicapping conditions since they are deprived of many of the sensory inputs they grow in a way which is unique to them. They perceive their self abilities, feelings, worth and values in a way which is quite different to normal ones. Over the last two decades attempts have been made to study the "concept of self" of the physically challenged children. Research reports till date do not document any study on the talented exceptional children focusing on their "perception of self." However, few research findings conducted abroad on "self-concept" of the children with handicapping conditions are presented below.

Karper, William B. and Martinek, Thomas J. (1982) assessed the differential influence of student's expressions of effort, school, teacher's expectations, sex, being handicapped/non-handicapped, grade, teachers, and race on the self-concept of the handicapped and non-handicapped children. The results showed that subjects expressions of effort had the strongest influence on self-concept, followed by school and teacher's expectations of subjects' ability to reason.

Koelle, William H. and Convey, John J. (1982) examined the relationship of self-concept and locus of control with the achievement of deaf adolescents. Generally, parent's hearing status and self-concept were the most important predictors of achievement. An increase in the prediction of achievement resulted when the modified forms of the scales were used in place of the original forms. This increase was due particularly to the locus of control variable.

Kelly, Kelvin R. and Colangelo, Nicholas (1984) stated that academic ability would be positively related to both academic and social self-concepts. In their study, conducted on gifted, general and special students, it is reported that subjects held significantly higher academic and social self-concepts compared to non-gifted age mates. Males with special learning needs scored significantly lower than other males on all scales.

Rich, Yisrael, Linor, Miriam and Shalev, Miriam (1984) studied on perceptions of school life among physically disabled mainstreamed pupils. Three groups were studied: extremely short, diabetic, and orthopaedically impaired children. Significant differences between the groups were found. Short subjects as compared to orthopaedically handicapped subjects were most satisfied with social aspects of schooling but reacted less positively to their teachers. Diabetic subjects were also less satisfied with their teachers than were orthopaedically handicapped subjects — and they demonstrated relative dissatisfaction with affective components of schooling. The study concluded that subjects did not form a monolithic group in their perceptions of school life and that unique reactions to schooling were characteristic of each group.

Maag, John W. and Rutherford, Robert B. (1986) conducted a study on behaviourally disordered, learning-disabled and non-labelled students and investigated perceptions of their behaviour as measured by the association between student and teacher rating scores on "student behaviour inventory". Results indicate that non-labelled and behaviourally disordered subjects were fairly accurate in the degree to which they perceived their behaviour when compared to their teachers' perceptions. Learning disabled subjects perceptions of their behaviour appeared less accurate. There was a significant difference in the relationship between student and teacher perceptions of the non-labelled and behaviour disordered groups.

Kistner, Janet, Haskett, Mary, White, Karen and Robbins, Frank (1987) conducted a study on perceived competence and self worth of learning disabled and normally achieving students. Learning disabled subjects held lower opinions of their cognitive abilities than did normal subjects. Compared to their peers, learning disabled subjects held less favourable perceptions of their physical abilities. Learning disabled and normal subjects ratings for general self esteem did not differ, nor did they vary in perception of social competence. Result indicated that learning disabled children maintain generally positive self-evaluations, despite their recognition of limitations in some areas. Based on comparisons between teacher and student ratings, subgroups of learning disabled subjects who held unrealistically positive or negative perceptions of themselves were identified.

Stephen, N. (1988) assessed the academic and social efficacy beliefs of the mildly handicapped, gifted and non-handicapped students. The study showed that the mainstreamed mildly handicapped students reported lower academic and social efficacy than their non-handicapped and gifted peers. No differences in academic self efficacy were reported between gifted and non-handicapped subjects. However, gifted subjects reported lower self efficacy beliefs than non-handicapped subjects.

Tilzer, Penny A. (1989) researched on the self-perceptions of special education students in special classes and the same age groups of special education students in regular education classes. Responses given by special education students in special education classes were much more negative than those by special education subjects in regular education classes, suggesting that the self-perceptions of labelled individuals may be negatively affected.

Grolnick, Wendy S. and Ryan, Richard M. (1990) conducted a study entitled self-perceptions, motivation and adjustment in children with learning disabilities and examined the self-perceptions, motivational orientations and classroom adjustment of children with learning disabilities, matched I.Q. non-learning disabled randomly selected non-learning disabled and low achieving children. The study showed that subjects with learning disability were lower in perceived cognitive competence, and academic self regulation relative to the non-disabled control group, but were comparable to the low achieving subjects. Subjects with learning disability were most likely to perceive academic outcomes as controlled by powerful others. Teacher ratings of subjects with LD were more discrepant from those of comparison groups than were self ratings of subjects with learning disability.

Bear, George G., Clever, Andrew and Proctor, Willison. A. (1991) conducted a study on self-perceptions of non-handicapped children and children with learning disabilities. The study showed that self-perceptions of scholastic competence, behavioural conduct, and global self worth of the learning disabled children are lower than the non-handicapped students. The study suggests that integration is unlikely to have a positive effect on the self-perceptions of children with learning disabilities.

Clever, Andrew, Bear, George G. and Juvonen, Jaana (1992) did a study on "discrepancies between competence and importance in self-perceptions of children in integrated classes" and examined self-perceptions of specific domains of competence, judgements of the importance of these domains and perceptions of global self worth among children with learning disabilities, with low achievement and with normal achievement. As measured on the self-perceptions profile for children, subjects with learning disabilities and lower achievement held lower self-perceptions of scholastic competence than subjects with normal achievement, and subjects with learning disability had lower self-perceptions of behavioural conduct than subjects with lower achievement and normal achievement. Both subjects with learning disabilities and subjects with lower achievement had significantly larger discrepancies between perceived competence and importance in the scholastic domain than did subjects with normal achievement. There was little evidence that subjects with learning disabilities employed a discounting mechanism to protect their self worth. There were no differences in feelings of global self worth.

Marsh, Harbert W. (1992) reported a high correlation between academic self-concept and academic achievement. It was also reported that self-concept and academic achievement relations were very specific to particular school subjects. The findings indicate that components of academic self-concepts are more differentiated than are achievement scores and that relations between academic self-concept and academic achievements are more content specific.

Vaughn, Sharon, Hagger, Diane; Hagan, Anne and Kouzekanani, Kamiar (1992) conducted a study to explore self-concept and peer acceptance in students with learning disabilities. The study suggested that learning disabled student's self-perceptions are not negatively affected by academic and social difficulties in the early grades or by identification and labelling process.

Bear, George G, Juvonen, Jaana and McInerney, Frances (1993) conducted a study on self-perceptions and peer relations of boys with and without learning disabilities in an integrated setting. The study showed that learning disabled boys showed lower self-perceptions of scholastic competence but not lower self-perceptions of social acceptance. Overall result suggested that although boys with learning disabilities in integrated setting often experience peer rejection and negative self-perceptions in several domains, they manage to maintain adequate self-perceptions of social acceptance by having a few close friends.

Coyner, Lisa (1993), investigated three constructs hypothesized to contribute to deaf and hard of hearing students success in mainstream settings: self-concept; social acceptance, and perceived social acceptance. Hard of hearing and deaf subject's self-concepts and their perceptions of their social acceptance were not significantly different from hearing subject's self evaluations. Hard of hearing and deaf subject's self-concepts were inversely related to the peer acceptance rating they received from their hard of hearing and deaf peers. The best predictor of academic success for hard of hearing and deaf students was the peer acceptance rating they received from hearing students. Thus hard of hearing and deaf student success in a mainstream program may be influenced by the social acceptance among hearing peers.

Sale, Paul and Carey, Dorism (1995) investigated the sociometric status of 592 children with disabilities in kindergarten by using positive and negative peer nominative techniques. Result showed that a combination of currently eligible students and candidates for special education had significantly lower social preference scores and higher social impact scores than did their general education peers. Among the groups subjects showed lower social-preference scores than those of general education students.

Cartledge, Gwendolyn; Cochran, Lessie and Paul, Peter (1996) examined the social adjustment of 37 female and 37 male students with hearing impairment with average intelligence. Subjects in mainstreamed settings consistently rated their social competence higher than those in residential settings, achieving significance on the category of self control. Girls consistently gave themselves higher self evaluation than boys.

Crocker, Alison D. and Orr, R. Robert (1996) investigated the social behaviours of children with visual impairment in a variety of pre-school settings. Subjects were nine visually impaired children and matched comparison group of nine sighted children. Observational data showed that the total number of interactions in both groups was similar. In the frequency of social initiation and the targets of initiations (teacher vs peer) made by students, however, differences were noted. Students were also likely to be recipient of an initiation, especially from a teacher.

Hagborg, Winston J. (1996) assessed the self-concept of middle school students with learning disabilities. The study focused on three low, medium and high sub-groups of V to VIII graders with learning disabilities on the basis of their self-reported ratings on the self-perception profile for children's (SPPC) Scholastic Competence sub-scale. An equal number of normally achieving subjects also participated. Correlations between the scholastic competence sub-scale and other SPPC sub-scales for both learning disabled and normally achieving subjects indicated a high degree of similarity between these two groups. There were significant differences between the low and both the medium and high sub-groups on internal locus of control for positive events, school attitudes and global self worth.

Rathman, Howard R. and Cosden, Merith (1996) investigated the relationship between self-perceptions of a learning disability and severity of a learning disability, global self-concept, domain - specific self-concepts, and perceived social support. Result showed that children with less negative perceptions of their learning disability had higher math-achievement scores and perceived a more positive global self-concept and more intellectual, behavioural, and social competence. These students also felt more support from their parents and classmates.

Stinson, Michaels; Whitmore, Kathleen and Kluwin, Thomas N. (1996) investigated the self-perceptions of social relationships in hearing impaired adolescents. The study showed that, in general, students reported participating in school activities more frequently with hearing impaired than with hearing impaired peers, but this was qualified by the extent that the students were mainstreamed. Ratings of participation with hearing impaired peers decreased for the students who were mainstreamed for more classes. Students indicated that they were more emotionally secured with hearing impaired peers, and there was increase in emotional security with hearing peers with more mainstreaming. Although these students were surrounded with hearing peers, this contact did not appear to promote identification and relational bonds with them.

King, Gillian A.; Specht, Jacqueline A.; Schultz, Izabela; Warr-Leeper; Genese et al (1997) examined changes in self-concept perceptions of support from close friends and classmates and loneliness in withdrawn unpopular children with cerebral palsy or spina bifida who had been involved in a social skills training program. Findings of the study indicated that group social skills training may be effective in decreasing feelings of loneliness and increasing perceptions of social acceptance in children who are withdrawn and unpopular at school. Subjects feelings of loneliness were associated with lower ratings of social acceptance and lower ratings of classmate support.

Farmer, Thomas W.; Rodkin, Philip C.; Pearl, Ruth and Van Acker, Richard (1999) conducted a study on teacher assessed behavioural configurations, peer assessments, and self-concepts of elementary students with mild disabilities. Seven configurations were identified for boys and seven for girls. The distribution of students with mild disabilities was examined across configurations. Fifty four per cent of boys and sixty four per cent of girls with mild disabilities were in configurations that may indicate adjustment problems or poor outcomes in adolescence and adulthood. Differences in peer assessments and self-perceptions of students with mild disabilities were examined in relation to teacher-assessed behavioural configurations.

Loeding, Barbara L. and Greenan, James P. (1999) examined the relationship between student's, self ratings and teacher's, ratings of generalizable skills of the sensory impaired students. Four sets of generalizable skills were studied. The findings revealed little agreement between the students and their teachers about the students' levels of skills.

Obozut, John E.; Maddock, Gerrard J. and Lee, Carolyn P. (1999) studied the effects of early language development, socialization and types of educational placement on the development of deaf and hard of hearing children's self-concept and did several compositions between hearing and deaf and hard of hearing children's self-concept. The study showed that deaf and hard of hearing individuals with deaf parents appear to have better self-concepts than deaf and hard of hearing individuals with hearing parents. The study suggested that deaf and hard of hearing students in residential schools have higher self-concept than their peers in regular public school classes. The study has focused on the problems associated with the measure of self-concept of the deaf and hard of hearing children which include inappropriate language structures, vocabulary requirements, and low test-retest reliabilities.

Gronmo, Siv Johane and Augestad, Liv. Berit (2000) conducted a study on "physical activity, self-concept and global self worth of blind youths in Norway and France." The study evaluated the differences between the levels of physical activity and efforts on physical and social self-concepts and global self worth between blind children in Norway and who attended integrated public schools and those in France who attended special schools. The study reported no significant differences between the blind Norwegian integrated and French special school youths in physical activity (except sit up) and anthropometric measures, skills and competence, physical and social self-concepts and global self worth. These results suggested that different types of school provisions do not seem as crucial as was expected.

Lindsay, Geoff and **Dockrell, Julie (2000)** conducted a study to explore the behaviour and self-esteem of children with specific speech and language difficulties. The result showed that the children's behaviour was rated as significantly different from the norm on both the SDQ and JRS, with the parents more likely to rate the child as having problems, but also as having pro-social behaviour. Both teachers and parents tended to rate the boys as having more problems than girls on the S.D.Q. with significant differences for the parent's ratings occurring on the total score and the hyperactivity and conduct problem scales. The children had positive self-perceptions, which were comparable to the standardization sample, and generally significantly higher than those of the teachers. The language and educational attainment scores of the children in special and mainstream schools were generally not significantly different, but parents rated the later group as having more behaviour difficulties. Multiple regression analysis identified language comprehension and reading comprehension as the only predictors of the parent's rating of behaviour (on the SDQ). No relationship was found with the teacher's ratings (SDQ = Strength and Difficulties Questionnaire; J.R.S. = Junior Rating Scale).

Summary of the review of the above said sub-section

1. Researches focusing on exploration of self-concept of the talented exceptional children are few.
2. Of all the researches conducted on talented exceptional children the gifted learning disabled children have received most attention.
3. Comparison of self-concept of the children with handicapping conditions has been made mostly with their non-handicapped peers.
4. The mainstreamed disabled learners appear to possess low self-concept compared to their normal peers.

5. Orthopaedically impaired, visually impaired, and speech and hearing impaired children possess low perception of their self abilities, worth, feelings and values of life.
6. Teachers of these children possess low expectations from them.

Studies Relating to Learning Styles and Motivational Characteristics of the Talented Exceptional Children

Learning style, popularly known as a learner's characteristic approach to learn, represents an individual's important component of the learning process. Individual differences among learners is apparent. An individual's learning style is the translation of personality and cognitive style characteristics into study behaviour. Motivation is one of the primary, yet one of the most complex conditions essential to learning. A motivating condition causes a child to start, to continue, and to limit his activity on a particular task. Motivation in the general sense is a primary requirement in any learning sequence. Learning increases with increased motivation upto a certain point. Maximum gain in learning occurs at a moderate degree of motivation.

Researches conducted on the exceptional children and on the talented exceptional children depicting their learning styles and motivational characteristics are sketchy. However, few such research findings are presented below.

Johnson, Roger T. Johnson, David W. and Rynders, John (1981) compared the effects of cooperative, comparative, and individualistic learning experiences on the self esteem and perceived personal acceptance by the teacher of non-handicapped and severely handicapped students. Results indicated that those in the cooperative condition had higher self esteem and perceived more personal acceptance from the teacher than did subjects in the competitive and individualistic conditions. Handicapped students reported higher self esteem than the non-handicapped students.

Carbo, Marie (1983) stated that reading achievement improves significantly when students learn through their strongest modalities and supports the need for additional aptitude treatment interaction studies in this area. The study also stated that poor readers may, in part, have difficulty in learning to read because instruction has not accommodated their individual learning styles. Compared to good readers, poor readers tend to have a greater need for quiet, mobility, structure, informal design, interaction with peers and teachers, tactile, kinesthetic stimuli, and learning at a time of day other than early morning.

Dunn, Rita (1983) examined the environmental, emotional, sociological, physical, and psychological elements of learning style. It indicated that students can identify their own learning styles and verified that, (a) the increased academic achievement, (b) improved attitudes toward school, (c) reduced numbers of discipline problems that result when youngsters are taught through materials and strategies that complement their preferred learning styles. It also showed that gifted/talented students appear to be independent, internally controlled, self motivated, persistent, perceptually, strong, task committed, and non-conforming. Individuals with low reading achievement preferred an informal environment when studying or learning, were more adult motivated than self motivated, functioned best in the late morning, and preferred learning through their tactile and kinesthetic senses.

Griggs, Shirley A, (1984) discussed that based on the recent research which indicates that gifted and talented students have a core of learning style preferences that distinguish them from other students, it could be stated that they are independent (self) learners, internally controlled, persistent, perceptually, strong, non-conforming, and highly motivated. Techniques and strategies can focus on highly cognitive processing, reasoning, abstract thinking, creative problem solving, and self monitoring. It is concluded that within any group of gifted and talented students there are differences as well as similarities.

Smith, Linda H. and Renzulli, Joseph S. (1984) reported that since learning style matching has a positive impact on student achievement, interest, and/or motivation, learning style measures can be used to provide teachers with objective data. It is suggested that there is no definitive teaching approach and that a wide range of teaching styles will improve the quality of instruction. Assessment can help teachers direct their attention to strategies that are most effective with either individuals or small groups of students.

Paris, Scott. G. and Oka, Evelyn R. (1986) stated that self-regulated learning should be an educational objective for handicapped children and unsuccessful students. Self-regulated learning combines cognitive skill and motivational will so that students can select challenging tasks, apply effective learning strategies, and measure their success against personal standards. Self-regulated learning builds confidence in children and enables them to acquire effective problem-solving skills that extend beyond the classroom. Classroom programs that enhance children's learning strategies, meta cognition, and motivation as stated in the study are cooperative learning, conditional knowledge, comprehension strategies and self-control training.

Dunn, Rita, and Griggs, Shirley A. (1989) attempted to make a comparison of the learning styles inventory profiles of children form diverse cultural backgrounds, which revealed clear differences among the groups in the patterns of strategies the students reported. It is suggested that individual vs group characteristics should be addressed when providing instruction, regardless of cultural or racial background.

Deci, Edward L; Hodges, Rosemary; Pierson, Louisa and Tomassone, Joseph (1992) conducted a study on "autonomy and competence as motivational factors in students with learning disabilities and emotional handicaps". The study attempted to assess student's self-perceptions and perceptions of home and classroom contexts. Student's achievement and adjustment were predicted from motivationally relevant self-perception of context variables. Different patterns of relations emerged from the learning disabled and emotionally handicapped students. Competence and involvement variables were not central for learning disabled students and autonomy and support of autonomy were central for emotionally handicapped students.

Short, Elizabeth J. (1992) worked on normally achieving learning-disabled, and developmentally handicapped students and measured their cognitive, metacognitive and affective differences and to know about how much do they affect school achievement. It was found that normally achieving subjects were superior to handicapped peers in all domains; learning disabled subjects performed comparably better to developmentally handicapped students in all domains except cognitive and metacognitive. The pattern of relations between these domains and achievement was not uniform among the populations. Intelligence and ratings of cognitive competence were strongly related to achievement for learning disabled subjects. Achievement was strongly related to metacognition and adaptive language for developmentally handicapped subjects.

Yong, Fung Lan and McIntyre, John D. (1992) investigated whether group, gender and grade differences existed in the learning styles of learning disabled and gifted students. The study revealed group differences in preferences for light, design and kinesthetic modality and in motivation, persistence, responsibility and parent-teacher motivation. Gender and grade differences were found in preferences for mobility and afternoon learning respectively. Findings imply that incorporating the learning styles of both groups is important for individualized educational programming.

Erin, Jane N; Corn, Anne L. and Wolffe, Karen (1993) examined the learning and study skills of 106 high school visually impaired students. The study found differences only by the students GPAS, not by their preferred reading medium, type of school placement or plans to attend college. The strategies used by students with visual impairments were found to be similar to those used by sighted students.

Rottenberg, Claire J. and Searfoss, Lyndon W. (1994) analyzed data from a qualitative study on the literacy development of pre-school hard of hearing and deaf children to discover how the children learned to read, write, and spell or finger spell their names. Analysis revealed that children learned that names are powerful expressions of identity through teacher demonstrations, immersion in a literacy rich environment, and numerous opportunities to explore written language.

Schirmer, Barbare R. (1995) attempted to determine whether mental imagery could be used as meta cognitive reading comprehension strategy by elementary level deaf children. Subjects were nine severely and profoundly deaf children. Results showed that when subjects were encouraged to engage in mental imagery, they exhibited four qualities of thinking during and after reading which were identified as recollection, representation, inference and evaluation.

Lyxell, Bjorn; Holmberg, Ingegerd (2000) conducted a study on visual speech reading and cognitive performance in hearing impaired and normal hearing children on a sentence-based speech reading task and on a visual-visual word decoding task, but not on a word discrimination task. Differing from the case of adults, most cognitive tasks proved to be significantly related to sentence based speech reading performance, where working memory capacity and visual word decoding skill proved to be strongest predictors.

Summary of the review of above said sub-section

Review of this sub-section depicts the following:

1. The gifted/talented orthopaedically impaired, visually impaired and speech and hearing impaired children possess advanced, expressive elaborative vocabulary and may read prior to school entry.
2. They memorize and recall learning task and information easily.
3. These children are aware of cause and effect relationships and can question and apply information.
4. They appear to be divergent thinkers, can generalize and provide more than one correct answer.
5. They have prolonged attention span and are persistent.
6. They seem to be curious and possess many interests.
7. They want to take risks in achieving learning goals.
8. They display a sense of humour.

Studies Conducted in India

Research on children with special learning needs in India got its momentum during the last two decades of the 20th century. The limited research activity in this area has provided a very little spectacular outcome. Focus is yet to be given on the orthopaedically impaired, visually impaired and speech and hearing impaired children with potential gift/talent. Not a single study in India could be traced depicting perception of self, learning styles and motivational characteristics of the talented exceptional children.

The section given below, however, attempts to explore the self-concept, learning styles and motivational characteristics of the children with special learning needs.

Singh, S. D. (1983) explored the need patterns, achievement and adjustment of mentally superior children. The study aimed at comparing the need patterns of mentally superior children with those of average children. The study reported that:

(i) Need patterns, achievement, and adjustment in five areas (social, emotional, health, home and education) had a low positive relationship.

(ii) Superior girls had better adjustment in social and sexual attitudes,

(iii) High intelligent subjects belonged to high and upper middle social economic status categories,

(iv) There was a positive relationship between intelligence and achievement for the superior group but a negative relationship for the average group.

(v) There was a significant relationship between adjustment in four areas: health, home, social and emotional of superior as well as average children.

Pathak, A.B. (1984) conducted a study on disabled children in normal schools. The major findings of the study are:

(i) Most of the disabled children came from families with poor economic background.

(ii) Sixty-three of the seventy nine-children's fathers had studied upto higher secondary or below.

(iii) Parents of 46 children had a family income below Rs. 500/- per month.

(iv) Most of the disabled children were from large families having four to five children.

(v) The disabled children were somewhat reserved, emotionally stable, satisfactorily adjusted but low in

scholastic ability, demanding and easily excitable, obedient, expedient, vigorous and not very tense.

(vi) Overall adjustment was average. Emotional adjustment was good, social and educational adjustment was average.

(vii) Sociometric status was satisfactory.

(viii) Teaching was the most preferred pursuit while intellectual or political pursuits and material comforts received least preference.

(ix) Most of the children wanted to continue study upto post-graduation.

(x) The few problems which disabled children faced were fear of the school, difficulty with classroom learning, dissatisfaction with teachers, ridicule by other children and inability to participate in co-curricular activities.

Bala, M.A. (1985) conducted a comparative study of mental make-up and educational facilities for physically handicapped and normal children. The study reported that:

(i) Deaf, blind and orthopaedically handicapped children differed significantly from normal children in personality traits and values.

(ii) The physically handicapped children were reserved, stiff, detached emotionally less stable, submissive, serious, with weak superego, with-drawn, dependent, more shy, and apprehensive.

(iii) Deaf children were deliberate, inactive, phlegmatic, prudent and tender minded.

(iv) In values deaf children were less theoretical, economical, aesthetic, religious, political and more social.

(v) The deaf children were less intelligent.

(vi) The adjustment of deaf children was socially, emotionally and educationally less stable. They had poor home and health adjustment.

(vii) Blind children were restrained, worried and untidy. They were less economical and religious but had more social and aesthetic values.

(viii) Blind children possessed poor ideal, social and perceived self-concept.

(ix) Blind children had poor home, health, emotional and educational adjustment.

(x) Orthopaedically handicapped children were affected by feelings. They were obedient and untidy.

(xi) In values, orthopaedically handicapped children were less theoretical, less economical, less religious and more social and aesthetic. Orthopaedically handicapped children had a poor concept of their power and strength, and had more negative tendencies.

(xii) The orthopaedically handicapped children were less intelligent, had poor home, health, emotional, educational and social adjustment.

(xiii) The facilities available in the institutions for handicapped children were quite inadequate as compared with those provided in the schools for normal children.

Lata, K. (1985) studied on impact of parental attitude on social, emotional and educational adjustment of normal and handicapped students. Major findings of the study were:

(i) The parental attitude did not differ for normal and handicapped students.

(ii) The attitude of fathers and mothers of normal and handicapped students did not differ significantly for boys and girls.

(iii) Normal children showed a significant difference from handicapped children in adjustment.

(iv) Normal boys and handicapped girls showed better emotional adjustment than normal girls and handicapped boys.

(v) Normal students did not differ significantly from the handicapped in the field of social adjustment.

(vi) Normal students differed significantly from the handicapped students in the field of educational adjustment.

(vii) Parental attitude did not significantly affect the adjustment of normal students.

(viii) The attitude of parents affected significantly the adjustment of handicapped girls but did not affect the adjustment of handicapped boys.

Mathur, Abha (1985) did a comparative study of the adjustment problems, levels of aspiration, self-concept and academic achievement of crippled children and normal children. The major findings of the study were:

(i) Crippled children differed significantly from normal children in school adjustment, emotional adjustment and total adjustment. However, when comparison was made separately for boys and girls, it was found that crippled boys differed significantly in social adjustment only while crippled girls differed significantly from normal girls in social adjustment, emotional adjustment, and total adjustment.

(ii) Significant differences were found between crippled children and normal children, crippled boys and normal boys and crippled girls and normal girls in the level of aspiration measured in terms of goal discrepancy score.

(iii) Crippled children, crippled boys and crippled girls differed significantly from normal children, normal boys and normal girls in self esteem as well as in social esteem.

(iv) When academic achievement of crippled children, boys and girls was compared with that of normal children, boys and girls respectively, no significant difference was found between them.

(*v*) About 20-84% of the crippled children were found to be facing various educational problems.

Pandey, R.N. (1985) conducted a study on affectional deprivation, ego strength and adjustment pattern among visually handicapped children and their rehabilitation. It was aimed to make a psychological study of affectional deprivation, ego strength, and adjustment among visually handicapped children and their rehabilitation. The study reported that:

(*i*) The deprivation as felt by rural blind children was significantly more acute than that felt by urban blind children

(*ii*) There was no significant difference in the pattern of affectional deprivation between congenitally blind children and postnatally blind children.

(*iii*) Ten blind children had poor ego strength and poor adjustment. Emotionally they appeared immature and hence there was need for their rehabilitation.

Banerjee, N. (1988) investigated the adjustment of blind students in secondary schools. More blind students were found to be maladjusted than the sighted. Nearly one in five students had a moderate level of maladjustment with home environment, school environment and peers of the opposite sex. Surprisingly, the percentage of blind children maladjusted to home environment was one and a half times more than to school environment. How much it was due to home environment, how much due to segregation in special schools of the blind is a moot question.

Khan, A.H. (1988) covering a study on blind children concluded that these children were less achievement oriented, self-reliant and attribute failure to achieve themselves. They were found to be more self-centred, neurotic and withdrawing.

Upreti, V. (1988) reported lower self-concept in children with orthopaedic impairments. The students with physical impairments felt more insecure and had poor adjustment. The girls felt more insecure than boys. These characteristics are related to the severity of disability. Like visually handicapped they relate poorly to parents.

Sharma, P. (1989) reported lower linguistic competence in hearing impaired children as compared to children with normal hearing. Within hearing impaired children, those studying in regular schools had higher linguistic competence than those in regular schools for the deaf. Differential analysis for different degrees of hearing impairment and causes for higher linguistic competence in integrated settings could make the feelings more meaningful. The studies point to special needs but do not specify for classroom practice.

Tiwary, Poonam and Verma (1989) reported positive attitude towards children with disability in families which had access to information and had knowledge about potentialities and limitation.

Fischgrand, J.E. (1990) lamented the lack of research in instructional methodology for education of the deaf children though efforts concentrated on assessment of an communication with them.

Kapoor, S. (1990) studied cognitive functioning and perspective taking ability of hearing impaired children. Parental behaviour inventory, facial expression test to assess perspective taking, Koh's Block Design Test, Alexander's Pass Along Test, terminal examination scores and teacher's rating scales were used. The two groups differed on Pass Along, and Koh's Block Design Tests. Institutionalized deaf children perceived parents more accepting than non-institutionalized ones. The institutionalized and non-institutionalized students did not differ in respect of perspective taking ability.

Sharma, I.P. (1990) studied the personality of low and high creative children with physical impairments. He reported no locational differences (rural-urban) in the two groups. The high creative group of children preferred arts, science, and technical work while the low creative group preferred crafts. The high creative group of students were more reserved, assertive, responsible, imaginative, self-reliant and relaxed than their low creative counterparts who were dependent and humble.

Mandke, K.N. (1991) studied the effect of single modality stimulation on speech and language development of hard of hearing children. The study reported that teaching using a single stimulation modality in carefully structured individualized approach enhanced the development of language skills in hearing impaired children.

Mandra-Valli, M.R. (1991) discovered developmental log in visually handicapped children on cognitive development tasks. The study points to the special needs, for example, counselling of students and families in improving adjustment. Special effort is required to improve cognitive functioning to minimize the cognitive log. Cognitive training strategies should be tried out with these students.

Verma, B.P. (1991) conducted a study to find out the relationship between learning style and achievement motivation. The study supported that subject's learning style preference was independent of achievement motivation. In other words high and low achievement motivated students did not differ significantly in terms of flexibility, individualism, visual vs. aural learning style, field independence, attention span, motivation centeredness, or orientation to environment.

Bissa, Sushma; Singh, B.G. and Heloda, R.D. (1993) studied the self-concept of blind and normal students. The study reported that blind subjects were at par with the normal subjects on all dimensions of self-concept. Blind and normal students showed similar self-concept on all dimensions.

Bhardwaj, R.P. (1995) did a comparative study of personality factors among handicapped and non-handicapped children. The study reported that both the blind and the cerebral palsied children were more reserved as compared to non-handicapped children. Both the cerebral palsied and the blind children had lower mental capacity as compared to non-handicapped ones.

Kumar, Dinesh; Prasad, Sanjay Kant and Prasad, Birendra, (1995) conducted a study on adjustment patterns of physically handicapped. It was found that the normal and the handicapped subjects differed significantly in their home adjustment, social adjustment, emotional adjustment as well as in overall adjustment. The normal and the handicapped subjects did not differ significantly only on health adjustment.

Jyothi, D. Arun and Reddy I.V. Ramana (1996) did a comparative study of adjustment and self-concept of hearing impaired and normal children. It was found that the hearing impaired and normal children differed significantly in three areas; viz. health, emotionality and masculinity femininity, where hearing impaired children exhibited a better quality of adjustment in these three areas of adjustment than the normal children. The hearing impaired and normal children differed significantly in their self-concept. Hearing impaired children had low self-concept compared to normal ones.

Sinha, Renuka Kumari; Roy, G.S. and Sharma, Anuradha (1996) studied the sex differences among orthopaedically handicapped in relation to the perception of socio-emotional climate in school. The study reported that there was significant difference between orthopaedically handicapped boys and girls on social perception and emotional perception.

Asha, C.B. (1997) studied on creativity of hearing impaired and normal children. The study reported that normal and hearing impaired children differed significantly in creativity. Normal children were found more creative than hearing impaired children. No significant difference was observed between the normal and hearing impaired children in fluency. However, in flexibility the two groups of children seemed to differ significantly. Normal children were found to have larger scores in flexibility. The same trend was observed with respect to originality also. Normal children had a higher mean score in originality than the other group.

Bhardwaj, R. (1997) did a study on adequate depth of feeling and sex as correlates of the need for achievement among handicapped and non-handicapped children. It was found that adequate depth of feeling promoted the need for achievement in general and specially in non-handicapped boys and demoted the need for achievement in congenitally blind boys. The need for achievement was masculine in both non-handicapped children imbued with high level of adequate depth of feeling and in cerebral palsied children having high level of adequate depth of feeling. The need for achievement was feminine in congenitally blind children who were imbued with high level of adequate depth of feeling. In comparison to non-handicapped, the cerebral palsied children had greater need for achievement in general. In comparison to non-handicapped, the congenitally blind children had greater need for achievement in general and in those boys who were imbued with low level of adequate depth of feeling and in those girls who were imbued with high level of adequate depth of feeling. In comparison to cerebral palsied, the congenitally blind children had greater need for achievement in girls who were imbued with high level of adequate depth of feeling. In comparison to congenitally blind children, the cerebral palsied had greater need for achievement in those boys who were imbued with high level of adequate depth of feeling.

Pathak, Anjali (1997) conducted a study to asses the level of creative thinking abilities of visually impaired, hearing impaired and normal pupils. The study reported that children with normal physical capacities had significantly higher level of creativity than their visually impaired and hearing impaired counter-parts. Not only socio-economic status but school environment played a crucial role in developing creativity. So far as age was concerned it had been found that there was a progressive increase in creativity with the advancement of age but with a very little deviation which might be a chance factor.

Summary of the review of the above said section

1. Research conducted on the group of children with special learning needs in India is in its embryonic stage and has a very limited coverage of dimensions.
2. Most of the studies have focused on variables other than learning styles and motivational characteristics.
3. Not a single study exploring the psychological traits of the talented exceptional children could be traced.
4. Most of the study findings have been compared with their normal (non-handicapped) peers.
5. Attempt has not made to identify the potential gift and/or talent of the children with special learning needs.

Conclusion

After reviewing and summarizing the related literature regarding self-concept, learning styles, motivational dispositions and problems of the talented exceptional children, a need was felt to study various issues relating to the psychological make-up of the orthopaedically impaired, speech and hearing impaired and visually impaired children with potential gift/ talent. It was thought important to study the following:

1. Perception of self of the talented exceptional children.
2. Learning styles of the talented exceptional children.
3. Motivational characteristics of the talented exceptional children.
4. Teacher's perception of talent aspect of the exceptional children.
5. Relationship between perception of self, and learning styles and motivational characteristics of the talented exceptional children.

4

Methodology and Data Collection

The present study was undertaken after an intensive and extensive review of related literature that documents the fact that the physically challenged individuals with potential gift/talent constitute a distinguished sub-group. To study the psychological traits of the talented exceptional children, the researcher has focused on certain variables namely, perception of self, learning styles and motivational characteristics which were explored through various tools already existing as well as developed by the researcher.

In this context, the present chapter is devoted to discuss in detail the procedure and method of the study. This chapter is divided into the following sections:

1. Statement of the Problem
2. Aim of the Present Study
3. Objectives
4. Hypotheses
5. Plan and Procedure of the Study
6. Sampling Procedure
7. Research Paradigm of the Study
8. Tools
9. An Overview of the Procedure Adopted for Data Collection

Statement of the Problem

"A study of talented exceptional children in relation to their perception of self, learning styles and motivational characteristics".

Aim of the Present Study

The aim of the present study is to explore the perception of self, learning styles and motivational characteristics of the talented exceptional children and to suggest ways and means for nurturing the potential gifts and talents of this neglected sub-population which could be used by the future planners, educators and other related professionals of special education.

Objectives

1. To identify the talented othopaedically impaired, visually impaired and speech and hearing impaired children.
2. To explore the perception of self, learning styles and motivational characteristics of the talented orthopaedically impaired, visually impaired and speech and hearing impaired children.
3. To explore the differences among each of the three groups of talented exceptional children on the above-said three variables.
4. To find out inter-correlations among perception of self, learning styles, and motivational characteristics of each of the three groups of talented exceptional children.
5. To find out strength of predictability of teacher's perception of each of the three groups of talented exceptional children on the basis of perception of self, learning styles, and motivational characteristics.
6. To find out strength of predictability of perception of self of each of the three groups of talented exceptional children on the basis of learning styles and motivational characteristics.

Hypotheses

To achieve the framed objectives of the present study, several hypotheses have been formulated which are:

1. The talented orthopaedically impaired, talented visually impaired, and the talented speech and hearing impaired children possess (i) low perception of self, (ii) low achievement motivation.
2. The talented orthopaedically impaired and talented visually impaired children do not differ significantly on (i) teacher's perception, (ii) perception of self, (iii) preferred learning style(s), (iv) and on achievement motivation.
3. The talented orthopaedically impaired and the talented speech and hearing impaired children do not differ significantly on (i) teacher's perception, (ii) perception of self, (iii) preferred learning style(s) and on (iv) achievement motivation.
4. The talented visually impaired and the talented speech and hearing impaired children do not differ significantly on (i) teacher's perception, (ii) perception of self, (iii) preferred learning style(s), and on (iv) achievement motivation.
5. There is a positive correlation between teacher's perception and perception of self, teacher's perception and preferred learning style, and teacher's perception and achievement motivation of the: (i) talented orhopedically impaired children, (ii) talented visually impaired children, (iii) talented speech and hearing impaired children.
6. There is a positive correlation between perception of self and preferred learning style of the, (i) talented orthopaedically impaired children, (ii) talented visually impaired children, (iii) talented speech and hearing impaired children.
7. There is a positive correlation between perception of self and achievement motivation of the (i) talented orthopaedically impaired children, (ii) talented visually impaired children, (iii) talented speech and hearing impaired children.
8. Prediction of 'teacher's perception could be made on the basis of "perception of self", "preferred learning style" and that of "achievement motivation" of the (i) talented orthopeducally impaired children, (ii) talented visually impaired children, (iii) talented speech and hearing impaired children.
9. Prediction of 'perception of self' could be made on the basis of 'preferred learning style' and of 'achievement motivation'

of the (i) talented orthopeducally impaired children, (ii) talented visually impaired children, (iii) talented speech and hearing impaired children.

Plan and Procedure of the Study

The plan and procedure of the study has been presented below in two sub-sections.

Plan of the Study

The researcher developed the following plan with a purpose to fulfil the framed objectives and test the formulated hypotheses of the present study:

1. Construction of tools for identification of the talented exceptional children.
2. Identification of the sample of talented orthopaedically impaired, visually impaired and speech and hearing impaired children from various special schools in Delhi.
3. Construction of tools for the measurement of perception of self of the identified sample.
4. Identification of tools for exploring learning styles and achievement motivation of the talented exceptional children.
5. Collection of data on the sample after administering the different existing and self-constructed tools.
6. Application of different statistical measures i.e. 't'-test, simple correlation, simple, double and multiple regression equations so as to achieve the objectives of the present study and to test the formulated hypotheses.
7. Interpretation of the findings of various statistical measures and drawing conclusions.

Procedure of the Study

The present study is a piece of descriptive research. It surveys the psychological traits of the talented exceptional children in terms of their "perception of self", learning styles" and "motivational characteristics". Like any other descriptive study, it attempts to explore and interpret "what exists" with respect to the above stated variables. It is concerned with conditions, relationships that exist, opinions that are held, processes that are going on, effects that are evident, or trends that are developing.

The study deals with "perception of self", "learning styles" and "motivational characteristics", of the talented orthopaedically impaired, visually impaired, and speech and hearing impaired children. It provides a generalised picture of behavioural and learning characteristics of the three categories of talented exceptional children. Thus the study describes the existing status of the talented exceptional children with regard to the above said variables. The study therefore is a descriptive survey in nature and correlational in profile.

Sampling Procedure

The selection of sample of talented exceptional children followed the below given sequence.

Criteria for Identification

The operational definitions used in the present study define gifted and talented children are those identified by professionally qualified persons who by virtue of outstanding abilities are capable of high performance. Children capable of high performance include those with demonstrated achievement and/or potential ability in any of the following areas singly or in combination (a) general intellectual ability, (b) specific academic aptitude, (c) creative or productive thinking, (d) leadership ability, (e) visual or performing arts, and (f) psychomotor ability. Following this definition, a physically challenged child does not have to be superior in all dimensions in order to be considered gifted or talented. High potential or demonstrated achievement in only one area is sufficient for meeting the criteria of giftedness or talent.

The three most frequently used procedures for identifying gifted and talented children are teacher nomination, tests of Achievement and I.Q. tests (Cox, Daniel and Boston, 1985) supplemented with additional sources of information from parents and peers. Tests of achievement and intelligence are of limited use because most of these tests are standardised on normal (non-handicapped) population. Use of such tests may add a handicap to the discovery of giftedness or talent among the physically challenged children. Lupat (1990) recommends that information from multiple sources be drawn together to minimise the possibility of bias in any criterion, and to ensure a balanced holistic view of

Research Paradigm of the Study

Table 4.1: Research Paradigm of the Study

Variables under study	Initial sample	Final sample	Tools used		Scheme for data analysis
			Standardised	Constructed	
1. Teacher's perception			1. Learning style inventory by D.A. Kolb (1985)	1. Checklist for identification of the talented exceptional children. (For teacher's use)	1. Descriptive statistics
2. Perception of self	600 disabled children (orthopaedically impaired, visually impaired and speech and hearing imparied children)	"36" Talented exceptional children	2. Achievement values and anexity inventory by Prayag Mehta (1978)	2. Check list for identification of the talented exceptional children (For parent's/Hostel warden's use).	2. T-Test
3. Learning styles				3. "Self perception inventory" for measuring perception of self	3. Simple correlations
4. Motivational characteristics					4. Simple regression 5. Double regression 6. Multiple regression

the child. Hence, for identification of the sample for the present study following three dimensions were taken into consideration:

1. Teacher nomination,
2. Parents/Hostel wardens nomination,
3. Rating of the researcher.

For identifying the sample, focus has been given on three categories of physically challenged children namely, orthopaedically impaired, visually impaired, and speech and hearing impaired children.

Procedure Adopted for Identification

A list of all the special schools catering to the educational needs of the orthopaedically impaired, visually impaired and speech and hearing impaired children in Delhi was collected from Ministry of Social Welfare. The researcher visited each of these special schools and discussed thoroughly with special educators, principals and other related professionals regarding infrastructure of these schools keeping in view to ascertain the availability of the sample. Finally four special schools were selected from which the sample of the present study was drawn.

The names of the four special schools are:

1. Amar Jyoti Research and Rehabilitation Centre (A co-educational school for the orthopaedically impaired children).
2. Blind Relief Association (A school for the visually impaired boys).
3. Lady Virjananda Andha Kanya Mahavidyalaya (A school for the visually impaired girls).
4. Lady Noyace School (A co-educational school for the speech and hearing impaired children).

A brief description of the above said four special schools has been given here:

1. Amar Jyoti Research and Rehabilitation Centre

Amar Jyoti Research and Rehabilitation Centre is a privately run organisation, which has three units, namely, (i) Amar Jyoti

Co-educational Special School, (ii) Health and Rehabilitation Centre and (iii) Teachers' training centre. The health and rehabilitation centre provides medical services to the orthopaedically impaired individuals. The teachers' training centre provides training programmes to the would-be teachers of the physically challenged children.

Amar Jyoti Special School mainstreams the orthopaedically impaired children along with the normal ones. It is a co educational school and has classes from pre primary to standard VIII. The school houses large number of orthopaedically impaired children compared to their normal peers. The school is affiliated to the "Central Board of Secondary Education". The school has a very good premise with properly designed classrooms. It has an excellent library, well designed art and craft room, physiotherapy room and a play ground. Special educators take proper care of the children.

Besides, general education, the school imparts training in art and craft, music, dance and drama, physiotherapy and in athletics. The vocational training centre provides training in different trades keeping in view the interests and aptitudes of the students. However, the school attempts to help every student to achieve their all-round development.

Students of this school represent low, medium and high socio-economic strata of the society. Many of the parents of these children are either uneducated or little educated while few of them possess good education. Parents, like the special educators, take keen interest in educating their kids. The school is a model institute which not only caters to the educational and vocational needs of its students but also provides various related services. Many of its students have successfully participated and achieved medals in art and craft, music and sports both at national and international levels.

2. Blind Relief Association

Blind Relief Association is a Government-aided special school for the visually impaired boys. The school is recognised by the "Central Board of Secondary Education", New Delhi. The school follows the same recruitment policy as those laid down by the Government. Teachers of the school are properly trained to teach the visually impaired children. The school is graded from primary to class XII. Students of the school represent a large population so far as their chronological age and socio-economic status are concerned. Both parents and teachers take keen interest in educating the visually impaired children.

The classrooms of the school are well organised. It has a very good library and most of its collections are in braille. It has a very sophisticated music room where students take great interest in learning music. It has its own health care centre. The school's counselling centre provides educational and vocational guidance as well as counselling services by professionally trained persons to the needy children. The school provides special training both in sports and games. Students here play more or less the same games as played by the sighted ones. Many of its students have received awards at national level.

The school has got a well developed vocational training centre which provides training in different trades to its senior class students. The school has its own hostel that houses those students who basically do not belong to Delhi. Blind Relief Association is said to be a model institution for educating and bringing all-round development of the visually impaired boys.

3. Lady Virjanada Andha Kanya Mahavidyalaya

This is one of the good school for the visually impaired girls in Delhi. It is affiliated to Central Board of Secondary Education, New Delhi. It gets 90% aid from the Government and the rest is bore by the founder trust. It has two sections. The junior section has classes from Ist to Vth while the senior section has classes from VIth onwards. The researcher was confined to the junior section only.

The school does not provide integrated education facility. Special educators of the school are properly trained to look after the educational needs of the students. Besides special education, the school provides special training in music, games and sports. The students of the school represent a large population with regard to their chronological age and socio-economic status. The school conducts regular parent-teacher meetings to ensure the quality of education. Many of its students have successfully participated in national level game and sports competitions.

Quite a large number of students stay in the school's hostel attached to the school building. A homely environment prevails inside the school premise. The school provides all the facilities and security to its students which in turn help them to integrate into the larger society in future.

4. Lady Noyace School

Lady Noyace School, Delhi Gate, New Delhi, is a co-educational special school for the speech and hearing impaired boys and girls. It is run by Ministry of Social Welfare of Delhi Administration. The school is one of the best special schools in Asia for the speech and hearing impaired children. The school is affiliated to the Central Board of Secondary Education, New Delhi, and graded from Pre-primary to XII. It has separate sections for boys and girls. The school follows the same curriculum like other schools affiliated to CBSE. The school possesses separate science laboratories, music room, art and painting room. All its classrooms are conducive for teaching and learning purposes. The teachers of the school are properly trained to handle the speech and hearing impaired children. Besides special education, the school provides coaching in games and sport, training in art and craft, drawing and painting and in music. Students take active participation both in academic and co-curricular activities.

Students of this school represent a large population with regard to age, sex, and socio-economic status. Students at primary and pre-primary level are taught through the use of hearing aids and other related materials. The school conducts regular parent-teacher meetings. The school has its own separate hostels for boys and girls. The hostels are well organised and properly maintained.

Initial Sample Distribution

Following is the initial distribution of the sample after screening of the special schools.

Process of Identification

Separate lists of the concerned special educators of the chosen classes of each of the four special schools were prepared.

Table 4.2: Initial Sample Distribution

Sl. No.	Name of the special schools	No. of classes	No. of students	Total no. of students
1.	Amar Jyoti Research and Rehabilitation Center	6	180	
2.	Blind Relief Association	6	150	600
3.	Lady Virjananda Andha Kanya Mahavidyalaya	3	50	
4.	Lady Noyace School	6	220	

Group meetings with the special educators in each of the four schools were convened in order to orient them in the task of talent identification. Concept of "talented exceptional children" was clearly explained. The process of filling up of the checklist was displayed and they were requested to participate in the identification process.

Requisite checklists were provided to the special educators. Checklists thus filled in were scored by the researcher. The children who obtained maximum scores and were nominated by many of the special educators were initially identified as the talented exceptional children. In order to strengthen the identification process, parents/hostel wardens were asked to state their views regarding these children by filling up the checklists developed by the researcher. Besides, the researcher himself made subjective structured observation of these children in different situations like classroom, music room, art and craft room, and play ground. Creative products of these children like drawing and paintings, pictures, cartoons, models, composed poems and short stories were also evaluated by the subject experts.

Finally, on the basis of teachers nominations, parent's/hostel warden's nominations, researcher's own observation and taking into account the creative products of these children, a list of talented exceptional children was prepared which constituted the final sample of the present study. The sampling distribution of the talented exceptional children is shown in table 4.3.

Table 4.3: Final Sample Distribution

S. No.	Categories	No. of children	Total no. of Talented exceptional children
1.	Talented orthopaedically Impaired children.	12	
2.	Talented visually Impaired children.	12	36
3.	Talented speech and hearing impaired children	12	

Tools

The researcher made use of both standardised and self-made tools in the present study. In all, five tools were used, three of which were constructed by the researcher whereas the other two were already existing (standardised). These are:

1. Checklist for identification of the talented exceptional children (For teacher's use)—Constructed.
2. Checklist for identification of the talented exceptional children (For parent's and hostel warden's use)-Constructed.
3. Self-perception inventory (For measuring perception of self)—Constructed.
4. Learning style inventory-By D.A. Kolb (1985)—Standardised.
5. Achievement values and anxiety inventory—By Prayag Mehta (1980)—Standardised.

The detailed description of the tools are given below:

Tools For Identification

Rationale

Identification of the gifted and talented physically challenged children is not a routine procedure. A major problem is that their potential gifts or talents usually remain invisible to teachers and sometimes even to parents. Another problem is that the handicap itself may obscure the expression of the special gifts or talents. For example, blindness, deafness, and some learning disabilities have the effect of slowing the development and thus may result in lower intellectual capacity along with intelligence quotient scores. Similarly orthopaedic impairment, emotional disturbance and speech and hearing impairment also can interfere with an accurate and speech hearing impairment also can interfere with an accurate estimation of I.Q.

The I.Q. tests and achievement tests which have been standardised on normal children are not found appropriate for use with the physically challenged children. Such inappropriate tests may under-estimate potential ability in the physically challenged students. Identifying the true ability of a physically challenged child who cannot see, speak or hold a pencil presents a unique problem and a challenge to the educators.

The pioneers in the field of gifted/talented education, over the last two decades have developed different approaches for identification of the talented physically challenged children. To help the identification of the talented physically challenged children, Maker (1977) recommended that (a) physically challenged students should be compared with others who have the same handicap; and (b) characteristics that enable the child to effectively compensate for his/her handicap should be weighted more heavily. For example, if an orthopaedically impaired student cannot write, his compensating verbal and cognitive abilities are to be given more weight. If a student cannot speak, his written, artistic and creative talents should be examined.

Karnes (1978), while stressing on talent identification, in her widely accepted RAPYHT (Retrieval and Acceleration of Promising Young Handicapped Talented) model stated that the talented exceptional children could be identified through the use of the RAPYHT parent checklist and teacher checklist—these two checklists attempt to identify children's performance in six areas of giftedness, namely, intellectual, academic, creativity, leadership, visual and performing arts and psychomotor abilities.

The procedure used by Eisenberg and Epstein (1981) for the identification of the gifted physically challenged children involved the use of both I.Q. and achievement scores. They also used Renzulli (1983)'s rating scales, which focussed on learning, motivation, creativity and leadership traits of the physically challenged children alone with their performance in art, music, drama, and communication. They also stated that peer nominations and self-nominations should be taken into account for the identification of the talented exceptional children.

Karnes and Shwedel (1981), Karnes and Johnson (1991) developed a two-step method for identification of the talented exceptional children. The first step of identification involves the use of "talent screening checklist" which is designed especially for identifying the gifted pre-school youngsters with handicaps. The second step of identification involves guided observation of top 25 per cent children (as rated by parents and teachers through the use of checklists) in one or more semi-structured activities for talent identification.

Like Renzulli's creativity scale (1983) as mentioned earlier, the other creativity scales which are found suitable for identifying the gifted/talented physically challenged children are "PRIDE" 1982, GIFT (1976), & GIFFI (Davis, & Limm 1980, 1982).

There is a general agreement in the literature that modification of the screening and identification procedures commonly used for gifted/talented children is required to increase the likelihood of recognising potential gifts and talents among the physically challenged students. General guidelines for modification include comparison of the gifted or talented physically challenged children with their like peers not with the non-handicapped children, and modification in testing situations in order to enable the physically challenged children to be free from their own prejudices. The guideline also gives emphasis on the issue that the special educators need specific training in the characteristics of giftedness among children with handicaps in order to identify them.

After making a thorough review of the existing and available literature for the purpose of identifying the talented exceptional children, the researcher felt it necessary to develop his own identifying tools by listing the observed characteristics of the talented exceptional children from the available sources. The two checklists developed by the researcher for the purpose of identifying the talented exceptional children for the present study are:

1. Checklist for the identification of the talented exceptional children. (For teacher's use).

2. Checklist for the identification of the talented exceptional children (For parent's/hostel warden's use).

A detailed description of these two tools is given below:

1. Checklist for Identification of the Talented Exceptional Children (For teacher's use)

Description of the tool

The checklist prepared by the researcher for the purpose of identification of the talented exceptional children by the teachers attempts to list the observed characteristics of the above said children. Such characteristics are easily identifiable by the special educators of the orthopaedically impaired, visually impaired and speech and hearing impaired children generally in school settings. The items included in the checklist cater to six areas of talent, namely:

(*a*) general intellectual ability,

(*b*) specific academic talent,

(*c*) creative ability,

(*d*) leadership trait,

(*e*) visual and performing art (art and music) ability, and

(*f*) psychomotor ability.

At the initial stage of preparation of the checklist, the researcher drafted a plan listing the observed characteristics of the orthopaedically impaired, visually impaired, and speech and hearing impaired children. The items in the initial draft plan were presented in statements. Each statement of the initial draft plan represented one particular observable characteristic of the above said three categories of talented exceptional children, containing 85 items uniformly catering to the above-mentioned six talent areas.

The initial draft plan of the checklist after being prepared was placed before the senior Special Educators of various special schools of Delhi, psychologists and counselors of various child guidance clinics of Delhi, teaching professionals of Deptt. of Special Education, Jamia Millia Islamia, New Delhi and few other senior professionals of special education working in different Non-government organisations, in Delhi for seeking their suggestions regarding it's modification. Each item of the checklist were thoroughly discussed with them and their valuable suggestions were taken into account. On the basis of their reactions to different items of the initially drafted checklist, many were modified and rearranged. Also, the number of items were reduced from 85 to 65 in order to avoid ambiguity. Equal weightage was given to the distribution of the items pertaining to the previously discussed six areas of giftedness. Again the draft plan was shown and discussed them with the professionals mentioned earlier and the final draft was prepared. The finally drafted checklist, used in the present study for identification of the talented exceptional children (for teacher's use), carried in all 65 items.

Validity

The face validity of the test was determined on the basis of the judgements of the senior special educators of different special schools of Delhi, psychologists and counsellors of various child guidance clinics of Delhi, senior professionals of Special Education unit of Jamia Millia Islamia, New Delhi, and of Blind Relief Association, New Delhi. Besides, the students who were identified as talented were also identified by the hostel wardens/parents by using a separate checklist. This establishes also the validity of the checklist.

Procedure for Administration of the Tool

The present checklist is designed to identify the talented exceptional children by the special educators only. The checklist could be administered individually as well as in groups. The special educators were to read the instructions given at the top of the checklist followed by one example. The teachers were to indicate their degree of consent by putting a tick (√) mark against each item in any one of the column namely "Always", "Sometimes", and "Never". The checklist did not need any fixed time limit to be completed. The teachers were requested to consult the researcher if they were in any difficulty in filling up the checklist. At the end of the checklist a blank space was given to state one's personal views about the child whom he/she would identify as talented exceptional.

Scoring Procedure

As the items in the checklist were given in statement forms and arranged in a three-point scale, the special educators were supposed to indicate their degree of consent by putting a tick (√) mark against each item in any one of the given three columns, namely, "Always", "Sometimes" and "Never". The expressions like "always", "sometimes" and "never" weighted 3,2,1 or 1, 2, 3 depending on the favourableness or unfavourableness of the statement. The total score for each checklist was obtained by summing up the scores obtained on each item.

2. Checklist for the Identification of the Talented Exceptional Children (For parents/hostel warden's use)

Description of the Tool

The checklist lists various characteristics of the talented exceptional children which are usually displayed by the physically challenged children during the developmental period. Such characteristics are usually observed by the parents of a physically challenged child or by the hostel wardens, caretakers, if the child lives in the hostel. The different areas of giftedness on which the checklist attempts to focus are:

1. General intellectual ability:
2. Creative ability
3. Social traits
4. Visual and performing arts
5. Psychomotor ability
6. Academic achievement/performance.

An initial draft pan listing the observed characteristics of the talented orthopaedically impaired, visually impaired and speech and hearing impaired children was prepared. The items of the plan were presented in statements. Each item of the draft plan represented one characteristic of the talented exceptional children. The initial draft carried 75 items.

The draft plan was then discussed with senior special educators of various special schools of Delhi, Psychologists and counsellors of different child guidance clinics, professionals of special education unit of Jamia Millia Islamia, New Delhi, and hostel wardens of various special schools of Delhi. Each of the items of the checklist were thoroughly discussed with the above said professionals. On the basis of their suggestions, some items were modified and the number of items was reduced in order to avoid ambiguity. At the end, 65 items were included in the final form of the checklist. Equal weightage was given to the distribution of items pertaining to each area of giftedness as stated above.

Validity

The face validity of the checklist was determined on the basis of the judgements of the senior special educators of various special schools, psychologists and counsellors of different child guidance clinics, and senior professionals of special education unit of Jamia Millia Islamia, New Delhi. The present checklist was effective in identifying those children who were already identified as talented by their concerned special educators. This also establishes the validity of the checklist.

Procedure for Administration of the Tool

The checklist was designed to be administered individually only. The parents/hostel warden(s) were requested to read the instructions given at the top of the checklist before filling it up. The instruction was followed by one cited example. No time limit was given to fill up the checklist. The parent(s)/hostel warden(s), if found any difficulty in filling up the checklist, were free to consult the researcher. The parents(s) hostel/warden(s) were to give a brief evaluation of the child's performance in different areas (both academics and non-academics) in the space provided with the checklist at the end.

Scoring Procedure

As the checklist was arranged in the form of statements in a three-point scale, the parent(s)/hostel warden(s) were supposed to indicate their degree of consent by choosing any one out of the three responses, namely, "always", "sometimes", and "never". The expressions like "always", "sometimes", and "never" weighted 3,2,1 or 1,2,3 depending on the favourableness or unfavourableness of the statement. The total score for each of the checklist was obtained by summing up the scores on each item.

3. Researcher's own observation for identification of the Talented Exceptional Children

The students who were identified as talented exceptional children by the special educators as well as by the hostel wardens or parents were observed by the researcher to make the identification process more objective and effective. An unstructured observation was conducted for the same. The children were observed in different settings namely, classroom, playground, art and craft room, music room and painting room. Such an observation helped the researcher to ascertain the talent aspect of the initially identified talented exceptional children in different areas of giftedness.

On the basis of the above-stated procedure the final sample was drawn that comprised of 36 talented exceptional children, 12 catering to each area of disability, namely, orthopaedically impaired, visually impaired and speech and hearing impaired children.

Tools used for measuring perception of self, learning styles and motivational characteristics

1. Self-perception Inventory

Rationale of the Tool

The concept of self has been developed from the works of early psychologists, philosophers, sociologists, and anthropologists. The ways in which "self" may be described are practically limitless. However, the term in its literary sense refers to a particular individual, that is, a personality, we wish to single out from the rest of humankind. It is a term referring to a specific person and has been indispensable in the historical development of person as conscious and thinking entities. In the words of Burn the self-concept is an image which an individual has of "oneself". The term "self" is regarded as the point of reference for everything one does. It provides the central core around which all other perceptions are organised.

Human beings have always behaved in terms of some kind of understanding of the self. In the behavioural sciences, however, the use of the concept of self has often been questioned. During the last few decades, the self has been given serious attention as a basic tool in psychological theory and research. The writings of Allport, Ansbacher, Maslow, Snygg, Combs, Murphy, Rogers, Bertocci and Raimy emphasised the importance of the self in psychology and laid the foundation for later research. In the last few years there has been an enthusiastic rebirth of interest in intrinsic motivating forces and cognitive and symbolic processes, particularly with reference to dynamic importance of the self. Today many psychologists who have adopted the concept of self as a subject of vast body of theory and experimentation state that much of the psychological development of a person is bound up with the emerging sense of self. According to their views, whatever be the way of describing oneself, each person develops a large number of more or less discrete perceptions of self which he/she regards as characteristics of his/her being.

Perception of self profoundly influences what a person thinks and how he behaves. The discrete perception of self does not exist in the perceptual field as a simple enumeration of ways of seeing the self. Rather, the concept of self constitutes an organisation representing a person's own conception of himself in all complexity. This organisation is not a mere conglomeration of isolated concepts of self but a patterned interrelationship of all self-perceptions.

The influence of children's self-concepts on their psychological behaviour and overall adjustment has been widely discussed by many of the researchers. The perception of self reportedly influences the manner in which the children conduct themselves in the classrooms, on the playground, as they interact with other children, and to some degree determine their attitude toward authority figures such as teachers, school counsellors, psychologists and other adults in the school. Some researchers have found that if programs are designed to enhance the self-concept of disadvantaged children it would result in significant improvement in their behaviour and psychological functioning.

In the words of Cohen (1977), physical ability is the prerequisite "by which the physically challenged child may learn about himself. Physical ability could be said to be crucial to the way an individual becomes conscious of developing a unique separate identity. It facilitates conceptualisation by receiving stimuli, interpreting information and enabling response. It is also of paramount importance in the area of general mobility, maintaining body functions, and enhancing the whole early learning process of social interaction, the building of self-esteem, and achievement of life goals. Other people's perception of an individual and that individual's perception of himself/herself will be greatly affected by physical appearance as well as mental achievement. The physical component is such an important factor in the development of the individual, it could be argued that the physically challenged individuals as they lack many of sensory functionings, would be possibly be affected in the process of self-concept development. Here it is obvious to note that the tools designed to measure the "self-perception" of the normal children, if administered on the physically challenged children, may not explore accurately the "perception of self" of the later group. It is in this context the researcher in the present study developed a "self-perception inventory" after going through various tools on "self-concept" and taking into account the functional disabilities of the physically challenged children, specially the orthopaedically impaired, visually impaired and speech and hearing impaired children. Various tools on self-concept discussed for developing the present "self-perception inventory" are given below:

I. Self-perception Inventory (SEI): By William T. Martin (1972)

It is a twelve-factor test of personality. It carries two hundred items. It is basically useful for counsellors, psychologists, and for clinical personnel in their evaluation of therapeutic progress and related programming of clients in the school, community clinic, and mental health institutions. It carries items like:

1. I hardly ever argue with people
2. I have frequent bed dreams.
3. I think that I would like to conquer the world.
4. I enjoy going outside and being close to nature.

II. Self-Esteem Inventory (SEI): By Stanley Coopersmith (1967) School Form

This tool is designed to be used with the primary and secondary school children. The inventory consists of 58 items in statement forms each one followed by a two point scale; "Like me", "Unlike me". The items are spread over a broad range like:

1. Things usually do not bother me.
2. I can make-up my mind without too much trouble.
3. Kids always follow my ideas.
4. I often get discouraged at school.
5. I am proud of my school work.
6. I can usually take care of myself.
7. I am not doing as well in school, as I would like to.
8. I always tell the truth.
9. I get easily upset when I am scolded.
10. I always know what to say to people.

III. Academic Self-image Scale: By John Barker Lunn (1970)

The tool attempts to measure the child's views of himself in terms of the school work. It is in the form of assertive and non-assertive statements followed by three-point scale. The statements are:

	Hardly ever	Sometimes after	Yes
1. I get lots of sums wrong	—	—	—
2. My teacher thinks I am clever	—	—	
3. I sometime think I am not good at anything	—	—	—

IV. Self-concept Checklist: By Pratibha Deo

This checklist attempts to measure the global self-concept of an individual. Items in this checklist are given in adjective forms, representing different dimensions of self. The attributes of these dimensions are: intellectual capacity and emotional characters, social characters and aesthetic characteristics of an individual. The checklist attempts to measure different aspects of self of an individual like perceived self, real self, social self and ideal self.

These and various other tools helped the researcher develop his own tool for exploring the "perception of self" of the sample chosen for the study.

Description of the "Self-perception Inventory"

After making a thorough review of the related literature on talented exceptional children and their self-concept as well as the tools on self-concept, the researcher developed his own tool which was basically designed to measure the global self-perception of the talented exceptional children. The "self-perception inventory" attempts to focus on three areas namely: (i) academic self; (ii) social self; (iii) physical self which are detailed below:

(i) **Academic self:** The academic self explores the academic self-concept of a child. It reflects a child's perception about failure and success, preference for various subjects, perception about his or her ability and future performance, dependence or independence in the matter of study or work habits and above all academic ability.

(ii) **Social self:** This is the aspect of self, "as perceived in relation to others", but pertains to "others" in general way. It reflects a child's sense of adequacy and worth in social interactions in general. It also measures the child's perception of his or her own behaviour, moral worth and feelings of being bad or good.

(iii) **Physical self:** This aspect of self reflects one's views about his/her body, state of health, physical appearance, skills and sexuality. It also reflects a child's sense of personal worth, feeling of adequacy as a person, and the evaluation of his or her personality apart from the body or the relationship to others.

The "self-perception inventory" used in the present study carried 65 items catering to academic self, social self, and physical self. The items were presented in the form statements. The initial draft plan comprised of more number of items on academic self, followed by social self and physical self. The draft plan thus prepared was shown to the senior professionals of special education unit of Jamia Millia Islamia, New Delhi, research wing of Blind Relief Association, New Delhi, and to the faculty members of Central Institute of Education, University of Delhi, Delhi in order to seek their suggestions. Each of the items of the inventory was thoroughly discussed with the above said experts. On the basis of their valuable suggestions, few of the items of the inventory were modified, rearranged and the total number of items were reduced. This helped the researcher to give the final shape to the "self-perception inventory'. The items thus got spread uniformly to academic self, social self, and physical self. The final draft of the "self-perception inventory" carried 55 statements.

Reliability of the Tool

The reliability of the "self-perception Inventory" was calculated through split half method by applying the Spearman-Brown prophecy formula. The value thus obtained was found to be 0.69 (N=36).

Validity

Face validity: The face validity of the "self-perception inventory" was restricted to the judgements of the senior professionals of special education unit of Jamia Millia Islamia, New Delhi, Blind Relief Association, New Delhi, and faculty members of Central Institute of Education, University of Delhi, Delhi.

Procedure Adopted for Administration of "Self-Perception Inventory"

The "self-perception inventory" could be used individually as well as in groups. Since the physically challenged children possess many functional disabilities, therefore in the present study the inventory was administered individually in conducive testing situations. Before administering the inventory in every testing situation the subject was made to sit comfortable, feel free from any physical and environmental distractions and the following instructions were given.

"The "self-perception inventory" attempts to explore your perception of self. The items in the inventory are in statements given in a three-point scale; "Always", "Sometimes", "Never". You will have to listen to each of the items read out by me and show your consent by choosing any one out of the above said three responses. There is not any right or wrong answer. Your responses will be kept confidential. There is no fixed time limit for completing the inventory".

However, the speech and hearing impaired children were instructed to read out the items one after another carefully and to put a tick (√) mark against each item in the appropriate column to show their degree of consent.

The subjects were then asked to either listen to or read the items of the inventory and their responses were collected.

Scoring Procedure

As the inventory was in the form of statements arranged in a three-point scale, therefore, the subjects were supposed to show their responses either in "always", "sometimes", or in "never" column indicating the degree of consent. The expressions like "always", "sometimes" and "never" weighted 3,2,1 or 1,2,3 depending on the favourableness or unfavourableness of the statements. The total scores for each individual subject were obtained by summing up the scores obtained on different self areas, namely, academic self, social self, and physical self. Scores obtained by each individual in each sub-scale were also calculated separately for further analysis.

2. Learning Styles Inventory (LSI): By D.A. Kolb

Retionale

It has been generally accepted that educational attainment depends not simply upon the nature of the learning environment and the ability of the student, but also upon the individual's learning style. Research into the concept of learning styles has burgeoned in the past few years (Eison, 1984). In the words of Claxton and Ralston (1978), the term learning style refers to "a student's consistent way of responding to and using stimuli in the context of learning".

Dunn, Dunn and Price (1985) defined learning style in terms of individual student reactions to various elements of instructional environments, immediate environment, emotionality, grouping preferences, psychological characteristics.

However, in general terms, learning style refers to the dimension along which one can measure an individual's approaches to learning, ways of thinking which are qualitatively different from each other. It is one's way of learning or the method a student uses to solve problems he/she encounters.

Learning styles represent an important component of the learning process, one that is necessary to understand if we are to have a comprehensive picture of learning. The study of "learning styles" has obvious implications for the management of learning in the widest sense, whether in the classroom, or elsewhere, for if children or adults have their own characteristic ways of thinking, problem solving and learning, then there is some argument for attempting to tailor teaching to their individual approaches.

Learning styles have been primarily investigated from the cognitive and affective perspectives and in few cases from perceptual modalities. The various approaches developed over the last two decades for the study of learning styles are based on the work of David Kolb (1976, 1984, 1985), Schmeck, Ribich & Ramaniah (1977), Brown and Hayden (1980), Honey and Mumford (1982), Dunn, Dunn, and Price (1985), and Kolb and Smith (1986). However, out of all these, the "experiential learning theory" of David A. Kolb (1976, 1984) has received the utmost attention in recent years.

A pioneer in the development of learning style theory, David Kolb (1976) proposed a model which suggests that "learning style is a result of heredity, experience and present environment". This approach of Kolb attempted to reflect many characteristics of students including genetic coding, personality and environmental abilities. Kolb (1984) modified his previous theory and developed experiential learning theory in which he integrated the cognitive socio-economic factors with the previous ones. This model depicts a cyclical process that involves four stages of learning, namely, (a) concrete experience; i.e. an experience in the social environment; (b) reflective observation, i.e. an individual's reflection on the experience from a number of viewpoints; (c) abstract conceptualisation, i.e., the person compares the experience to previous life experience and builds a theoretical format on which to explain the latter experience; and (d) active experimentation, i.e., the individual tests his theory on the environment and subsequent to the consequences being anew learning cycle.

Thus the typology of Kolb's (1984) learning style theory included four phases of the learning cycle: concrete experience, abstract conceptualisation, reflective observation, and active experimentation. Based on these propositions, Kolb (1976) constructed his "learning style inventory", which was later on revised in 1985. The revised form of Kolb's learning style inventory (1985) is used in the present study for the purpose of identifying the learning styles of the talented exceptional children.

Description of Kolb's Learning Style Inventory (Revised form—1985)

D.A. Kolb's (1985) learning style inventory is a simple self-description test based on experiential learning theory, that is designed to measure one's strengths and weaknesses as a learner in the four stages of the learning process. It describes the way one learns and how he/she deals with ideas and day-to-day situations of life. Effective learners rely on four different learning modes: Concrete Experience (CE), Reflective Observation (RO), Abstract Conceptualisation (AC), and Active Experimentation (AE). That is they must be able to involve themselves fully, openly, and without bias in new experiences (CE); they must be able to reflect on and observe these experiences from many perspectives (RO); they must be able to create concepts that integrate their observation into logically sound theories (AC); and they must be able to use these theories to make decisions and solve problems (AE).

The LSI measures one's relative emphasis on the four learning modes by asking one to rank order a series of four words that describes these different abilities. For example, one set of four words is feeling, watching, thinking, doing, which reflects CE, RO, AC and AE, respectively. Combination scores indicate the extent to which one emphasises abstractness over concreteness (AC-CE) and the extent to which one emphasises active experimentation over reflection (AE-RO).

The LSI consists of 12 sentences with a choice of four endings. Each of the endings is a characteristic representation of an individual learning style. To complete the learning style inventory, the respondent, must rank order four sentence completions in a row, one each in the four columns corresponding to a learning mode. Column 1 is the CE scale; column 2 is the RO scale; column 3 is the AC scale; and column 4 is the AE scale. The respondent assigns a 4 to the phrase that describes how he learns best, assigns a 3 to the next best description, and so forth giving a 1 to the least descriptive phrase. The summing up of the four columns reflects each of the four stages in the learning cycle. Combination scores are computed next by subtracting the CE score from the AC score (AC-CE), and the RO score from the AE score (AE-RO). The combination scores measure the extent to which an individual emphasises abstractness over concreteness (AC-AE), and the extent to which an individual emphasises action over reflection (AE-RO), in learning. Using the combination scores, the inventory delineates four different types of learners: the diverger who relies upon CE and RO; the assimilator, who prefers RO and AC; the converger, who emphasises AC and AE; and the accommodator, who chooses AE and CE.

Reliability

The test-retest reliability of Kolb's learning style inventory has been found to range between 0.30-0.73 and split half method reports to be 0.80. Reliability of Kolb's LSI also has been found out by Freedman and Stumpf; Geller; and Atkinson which is shown below:

Test Retest Reliability Coefficient of Kolb's LSI

BY Kolb

Sample	Interval	N	CE	RO	AC	AE	AC-CE	AE-RO
Med. Stud.	3mo.	27	.48	.73	.64	.64	.61	.71
Grad. Stud.	3mo.	23	.48	.51	.73	.43	.51	.48
By Freedman and Stumpf								
Grad. Stud.	5wk.	101	.39	.49	.63	.47	.58	.51
By Geller								
Med. Stud.	31 days	50	.56	.52	.59	.61	.70	.55
By Atkinson								
Fresh-men	9 days	26	.57	.40	.54	.59	.69	.24

To support the reliability of the above-said tools Willcoxson, Lesley and Prosser Michael (1996) report that Kolb's learning style inventory possesses high degree of reliability, with coefficient alpha reliabilities ranging from 0.81 to 0.87.

Validity

(i) Construct Validity

Kolb's learning style inventory though was developed for use with college students, but is currently used with high school and junior high school students (Ferrell, 1983). Kolb in his original form conducted discipline based research to demonstrate the validity of learning style inventory. His sample comprised of students of Physical Sciences, Business Studies, Languages, Education, Philosophy, History, Mathematics and Economics. He attempted to examine the issue of gender difference in preferred learning styles. Kolb reported a tendency for females to emphasize concrete experience and males to emphasize abstraction in various disciplines. Other than this, the students of business studies and physical sciences preferred to be "Accommodative", while the students of Language, Education, Philosophy, History, Mathematics and Economics were found to be the divergent learners. This fact establishes that Kolb's learning style inventory possesses construct validity.

Kolb's views have also been shared by Katz (1988), who found that male Israeli engineering students scored high on the abstract dimension while her female Israeli occupational therapy students scored higher on the concrete dimension.

(ii) Concurrent Validity

To support the validity aspect of the learning style inventory Willcoxson and Prosser (1996) in a discipline based research found that the arts students possessed a significantly higher mean score on "Concrete Experience" and science students had a significantly higher mean score on "Active Experimentation".

In the present study the learning style inventory also has explored a significant mean difference between the talented orthopaedically impaired and visually impaired children on

"Active Experimentation" (AE); between talented orthopaedically impaired and speech and hearing impaired children on "Abstract Conceptualisation" (AC); and both on AE and AC styles of learning between the talented visually impaired and speech hearing impaired children. The above stated fact also establishes the concurrent validity of the learning style inventory.

Procedure of Administration

The learning style inventory could be administered individually as well as in groups. In the present study due to various functional disabilities possessed by the subjects the inventory was administered individually in different testing situations. The child in each testing situation was made to sit comfortably without facing any disturbance and was told to listen to the instructions/or read them carefully. After that, the following instructions were given.

"The learning style inventory describes the way you learn and how you deal with ideas and day-to-day situations in your life. Below are 12 sentences with a choice of four endings. Rank the endings for each sentence according to how well you think each one fits with how you would go about learning something. Try to recall some recent situations where you had to learn something new. Then using the spaces provided, rank "4" for the sentence ending that describes how you learn best, down to "1" for the sentence ending that seems least like the way you would learn. Be sure to rank all the endings for each sentence unit. Please do not make ties".

After giving instructions the items were read out carefully loudly by the researcher one after another and the responses given by the subjects were noted down in the appropriate columns. In case of the speech and hearing impaired children in collecting data help from the special educators was taken.

Scoring

Scoring was done by summing up of the ranks given to each of the learning phases. Total ranks obtained by each learning phase represented the total score for that particular learning style. It is in this way for each child four scores were obtained representing four styles of learning, namely, Abstract Conceptualisation (AC), Concrete Experience (CE), Reflective Observation (RO) and Active Experimentation (AE).

3. Achievement Values and Anxiety Inventory (AVAI)— By Prayag Mehta

Rationale and Description of the Tool

The study of human motivation has to do with analysis of various factors which incite and direct an individual's actions. The meaning of motivation had been a controversial subject among psychologists for some time. In the history of experimental psychology the problem of motivation and problem of learning have been intimately linked. The primary interest in the study of motivation is to identify and to understand the effects of all the important contemporaneous influences which determine the direction of action, its vigour, and its persistence.

Work on the measurement of human motive is of recent origin. Although several approaches had been developed for the study of human motivation, the recent two approaches are based on the work of McClelland (1961) and Atkinson (1961). McClelland and his co-workers sought the origin of achievement in studies of child rearing practices and the consequences of n-achievement in cross cultural comparisons which relate n-achievement to indices of economic development. McClelland and his associates adopted Murphy's Thematic Apperception Test (TAT) for the measurement of human motivation. Atkinson and his associates focussed on psychological theories of motivation as a means of understanding of need for achievement. Atkinson's conceptualisation of n-achievement differentiates between the motive to succeed and the motive to avoid failure, seeking to explain achievement in the light of his differentiation and the perceived probability of success in specific tasks.

Everyone has a desire to achieve but it varies from person to person. A person's desire for need for achievement may remain submerged unless it is aroused or stimulated by some stimulant.

Based on the work of McClelland, Mehta (1976) developed the test, "Achievement Values and Anxiety Inventory (AVAI)", which was primarily designed to measure the motivational dispositions of an individual.

The AVAI in all contains 22 items. These items are descriptive statements of situations depicted in pictures which were tried out for the development of a thematic appreciative measure of n-achievement. Each item is followed by six responses. These responses are also based on the stories written to TAT type pictures. The six responses represent achievement related motivation (AR); task related motivation (TR) and unrelated motivation (UR), catering equally to the three types of motivation. Respondents have to check one response to each item.

Difficulty and Discrimination Values of the Items

The items were selected on the basis of their difficulty and discrimination values. The difficulty value was the percentage of AR to each item, and the discrimination values were obtained through biserial correlations between the top and bottom 27 per cent of the total scores. The difficulty values of the selected items ranged between 25 to 70 per cent with the median difficulty at 42.83. The discrimination values ranged between 25 and 75.

Reliability

The reliability of the test as calculated by K-R(20) formula was found to be 0.67.

Validity

The test does not depict any direct measure of validity. Only indirect validity like theoretical validity had been emphasised.

Mehta's test has been widely used in India for measuring achievement motivation. Gokul Nathan (1972) used this to find out the achievement level of tribal and non-tribal secondary school children in Assam. Bhargava (1972) showed Mehta's Cards to be better measure of n-achievement than Mukherjee's sentence completion test.

That is why this test was selected by the researcher for the use of the present study.

Procedure for Administration

The test could be administered individually as well as in group. Since the sample of the present study comprised of the talented exceptional children, who lack many functional abilities, therefore, the test was administered individually only. The subject in a testing situation was seated comfortably, facing no physical and environmental disturbances and was given the following instructions.

"This is a test that attempts to measure your motivational characteristics. The items in the test are in statement forms. In all there are 22 items each one followed by six responses. You have to choose only one response. There is not any right or wrong answer. Your responses will be kept confidential and in no way will interfere in your academic endeavour. Listen to the items carefully read out by me, one after another and show your response accordingly.

After giving instructions the researcher read out the items one after another and the responses shown by the subjects were carefully noted simultaneously.

Scoring

Scoring was done as per the guidelines given in the scoring key of the test manual. The test yielded three types of scores, namely, achievement related scores, task related scores and unrelated scores.

An Overview of the Procedure Adopted for Data Collection

The procedure for data collection in the present study followed a number of stages. Before data collection the researcher learnt Braille reading and different sign languages in order to make effective communication with the visually impaired, speech and hearing impaired children. To study perception of self, learning styles and motivational characteristics, three tests were used in the study. Each of these three tests were administered individually in different testing situations. Following is the schematic representation of the different stages of data collection.

(A) Procedure for the Selection of Sample

Purposive selection of four special schools was done

(B) Procedure for Construction of Tools

(i) Tools for Identification

(a) Visits to different special schools

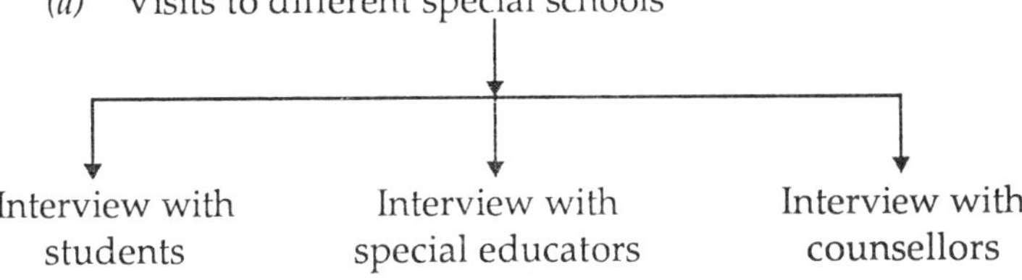

(b) Initial draft plan of the tools

(c) Visit to Blind Relief Association and Faculty of Education, Jamia Millia Islamia.

(d) Discussion and consultation with the professionals of special education with regard to modification of items of the initial draft plan.

(e) Modification of the items in the initial draft plan.

(f) Final form of the identifying tools.

(g) Tools ready for use.

(ii) Tool for Measuring Perception of Self

(a) Visit to different special schools

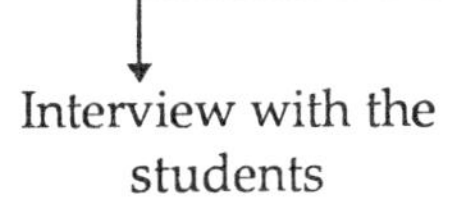

Interview with the special educators and counsellors

(b) Initial draft plan of the test items

(c) Visit to Blind Relief Association and Lady Noyace School

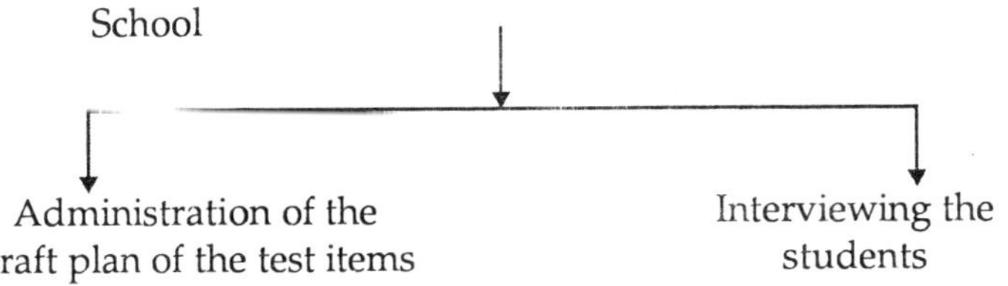

(d) Item analysis of the draft plan.

(e) Final form of the tool.

(*f*) Administration on the exceptional children.

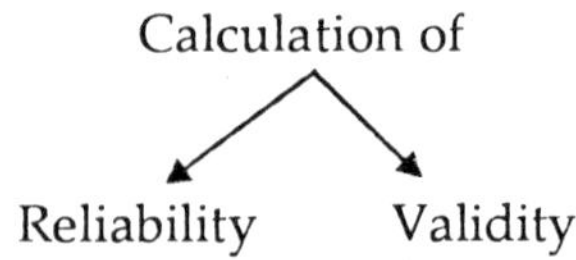

(*g*) Tool ready for final use.

(C) Procedure Adopted for Selection of the Final Sample

Selection of the final sample was made on the basis of:

(*i*) Teacher's nominations

(*ii*) Parent's/Hostel Warden's nominations

(*iii*) Researcher's self observation.

Final Sample

Sl. No.	Categories	No. of children	Total No. of children
1.	Talented orthopaedically impaired children	12	
2.	Talented visually impaired children	12	36
3.	Talented speech and hearing impaired children.	12	

(D) Procedure for Administering Tools for Collection of data

(*i*) Talented orthopaedically impaired children.

No. of children = 12

No. of tests administered = 03

No. of testing situations = 36 (12 × 3)

(*ii*) Talented visually impaired children.

No. of children = 12

No. of tests administered = 03

No. of testing situations = 36 (12 × 3)

(iii) Talented speech and hearing impaired children.

No. of children	= 12
No. of tests administered	= 03
No. of testing situations	= 36 (12x3)
Total No. of testing situations	= 108

The data collected as per the above said plan and procedure were put for statistical analysis and interpretation which has been presented in the next chapter.

5

Analysis and Interpretation

The aim of any research work is the discovery of general principles based upon observed relationships between and among different variables. It requires an objective, impartial and logical analysis of the data. Analysis of sample data helps not only in achieving the framed objectives set in the study but also in answering the projected questions. Since the present study is descriptive in nature, it is concerned with hypotheses formulation and their testing, analysis of relationships between different variables, determining the strength of predictability and drawing conclusions based on the findings of the study.

The present chapter highlights the analysis and interpretation of collected data. Analysis has been done with simple descriptive statistics followed by test of significance, inter-correlations, simple, double and multiple regression analysis. Both quantitative and qualitative approaches have been employed in order to have a holistic view of the findings. Interpretation, inter woven with analysis has given a coherent picture of the findings.

The following sequence in the form of different sections has been laid down for presenting this chapter.

1. Status Section
2. Statistical Comparisons
3. Correlational Studies
4. Regression Equations and Their Analysis
5. Summary of Findings

Status Section (status of the talented exceptional children on different variables)

This section deals with the status of the sub-groups of talented exceptional children on different variables. This section has been divided into the following nine parts:

1. Status of the talented orthopaedically impaired children on "teacher's perception" and on "perception of self".
2. Status of the talented orthopaedically impaired children on "learning styles".
3. Status of the talented orthopaedically impaired children on "motivational characteristics".
4. Status of the talented visually impaired children on "teacher's perception" and on "perception of self".
5. Status of the talented visually impaired children on "learning styles".
6. Status of the talented visually impaired children on "motivational characteristic".
7. Status of the talented speech and hearing impaired children on "teacher's perception" and on "perception of self".
8. Status of the talented speech and hearing impaired children on "learning styles".
9. Status of the talented speech and hearing impaired children on "motivational characteristics".

Status of the Talented Orthopaedically Impaired Children on "Teacher's Perception" and on "Perception of Self".

Table 1 shows the status of the talented orthopaedically impaired children on teacher's perception and on perception of self. A study of the table shows that teacher's perception of the talented orthopaedically impaired children is quite high and positive. It reflects that teacher's of this group show higher ratings about the talent aspect of these children. A look at the perception of self of the group shows that the group possesses low 'self' though found positive. A thorough study of "perception of self" reveals that among the three facets of self, the talented orthopaedically impaired children possess high academic self followed by social self but a low physical self.

Table 1: Status of the talented Orthopaedically Impaired Children on "Teacher's Perception" and on "Perception of Self"

Name of the variables	Sub areas of the variable	Mean score	Standard deviation	Variance	Minimum score	Maximum score
Teacher's perception	—	153.5	9.83	96.629	52	62
Perception of self	Academic Self (A.S.)	57.25	3.33	11.109	133	162
	Social Self (S.S.)	51.66	2.534	6.421	47	56
	Physical Self (P.S.)	13.66	1.614	2.605	10	16
	Total Self	**122.583**	**5.247**	**27.531**	**115**	**160**

An analysis of the responses made by the talented orthopaedically impaired children reveals that this group of children appear to be very much sincere towards their academic endeavour. They seem to possess good retention ability. They are desirous of showing academic excellence and are keen to learn more. They possess good attention span and ability to learn quickly the subjects they like compared to the unliked ones. They solve problems by using different strategies. Other than academic work they like to take part in drawing and painting, art and craft and in music but not in physical activities. They prefer freedom to discipline. They appear to feel boredom after doing monotonous activities. These children do possess a realistic perception about their failure and success in academic field.

A look at the 'social self' of the group shows that the talented orthopaedically impaired children possess the desire to know about the people around them. They want to gain varied experiences by making friends, taking part in social gatherings and cultural activities and exchanging views and ideas with others. They appear to experience greater difficulty in facing the socially accepted points of reference because they are different from other non-handicapped counterparts. Their perception of social justice is quite definite. Many of them want to excel in their leadership trait if proper opportunities were given. They seem to follow their own principles of life and not want to be disturbed by others. They are clear about their perception of success and failure in social life. They have highly developed aesthetic sense and appreciate the gift of the nature.

An analysis of the physical self of the group reveals that the talented orthopaedically impaired children are quite aware of their abilities and disabilities. They consider physical disability as a stigma but their future expectations are more positive than otherwise.

Status of the Talented Orthopaedically Impaired Children on "Learning Styles"

Table 2 shows the status of the talented orthopaedically impaired children on "learning styles". A study of the table reflects that each member of the group showed different preferences for each of the four learning styles. However, it is found that out of the four learning styles the group's first preference goes to "active experimentation' (doing) which is followed by "reflective

Table 2: Status of the Talented Orthopaedically Impaired Children on "Learning Styles".

Name of the variable	Sub areas of the variable	Mean score	Standard deviation	Variance	Minimum score	Maximum score
Learning Styles	Active Experimentation (A.E.)	37.166	4.628	24.418	29	44
	Concrete Experience (C.E.)	26	4.112	16.909	18	30
	Abstract Conceptualisation (A.C.)	24.75	6.224	38.738	13	34
	Reflective Observation (R.O.)	33.5	5.807	33.732	22	39

observation'' (watching), 'concrete experience' (feeling) and ''abstract conceptuatlisation (thinking)''. It depicts that the group's most preferred learning style is ''active experimentation'' i.e. doing and the least preferred learning style is ''abstract conceptuaisation'' i.e. thinking. It could be said that the group reflects a tendency to overemphasise on ''active experimentation'' at the cost of ''reflective observation'', ''concrete experience'' and ''abstract conceptualisation'' learning styles.

After analysing the responses it is felt that the talented orthopaedically impaired children learn new concepts and ideas by doing as well as by understanding the learning task depending on its nature. At the time of learning they emphasise on practical applications as opposed to reflective understanding. They are more pragmatic with regard to their learning approach. They are more result oriented. They are willing to take some risk to achieve their learning objectives. They enjoy and are good at getting things accomplished. They possess good span of attention. They rely on their own thoughts and feelings to form opinions.

Status of the Talented Orthopaedically Impaired Children on "Motivational Characteristics"

Table 3 shows the status of the talented orthopaedically impaired children on motivational characteristics. A deep study of the table reveals that the group possesses comparatively higher achievement related motivation compared to task related motivation. The group reflects avoidance motive. The group's AVAI score indicates that the group on the whole possesses low achievement motivation. An analysis of the responses shows that the talented orthopaedically impaired children because of limited body functioning appear to undermine their abilities and conceal their potential which indicates the existence of anxiety. It could be said that physical disability does influence in building up achievement motivation of the talented orthopaedically impaired children.

Status of the Talented Visually Impaired Children on "Teacher's Perception" and on "Perception of Self"

Table 4 shows the ''teacher's perception'' and ''perception of self'' of the talented visually impaired children. A study of this

Table 3: Status of the Talented Orthopaedically Impaired Children on "Motivational Characteristics"

Name of the variable	Sub areas of the variable	Mean score	Standard deviation	Variance	Minimum score	Maximum score
Motivational Characteristics	Achievement Related Motivation	10.66	1.56	2.42	9	15
	Task Related Motivation	6.33	1.07	1.51	5	8
	Unrelated Motivation	5.00	1.65	2.726	2	7
	Total AVAI score	**5.416**	–	–	**3**	**13**

Table 4: Status of the Visually Impaired Children on "Teacher's Perception" and on "Perception of Self"

Name of the variables	Sub areas of the variables	Mean score	Standard deviation	Variance	Minimum score	Maximum score
Teacher's perception	—	141.66	9.345	87.329	125	159
Perception of Self	Academic Self (A.S.)	53.166	3.43	11.78	47	57
	Social Self (S.S.)	49.166	4.195	17.598	45	56
	Physical Self (P.S.)	14.25	2.34	5.47	10	17
	Total Self	**116.166**	**7.918**	**62.69**	**102**	**124**

table reveals that teacher's perception of the group is high and positive. This indicates that the talent aspect of this group of children has been highly perceived by their teachers. A look at 'perception of self' of the group reveals that the group possesses low self though positive. A deep study of 'perception of self' of the group shows that the talented visually impaired children have better academic self compared to social self and have low physical self.

An analysis of the responses reflects that the talented visually impaired children possess strong desire for academic pursuit. They appear to be regular to school and very much sincere in academic endeavour. They take keen interest in learning and doing academic work sincerely. Other than studies they do take part regularly in sports and in music. In non-academic activities their most preferred area is music. They tend to possess high aspirations. They want to secure good grades both in studies and in cocurricular activities. They want to show excellence in future life. They express apathy towards strict discipline. They feel bored after doing same work repeatedly. They are quite sure about their future success. They have a clear perception of their academic abilities. They value patience and hard work. They argue that "success lies with hard-work". Their future academic expectations are quite high and positive.

With regard to "social self-perception" of the talented visually impaired children it is felt that like their sighted peers, these children display interest in making friends with others. They want to explore the world around them. They do experience restricted social integration. It might be because of the fact that they lack vision which is very much essential for perceiving the external world. These children do not feel easy in taking part in social gatherings and cultural activities. They do not share their feelings with sighted peers easily. They seem to advocate for the prevalence of love, care, security, and social justice everywhere in the world. However, these children do possess low "social self".

The physical self of the talented visually impaired children is found low. They appear to be quite sure about their physical abilities. Though they possess low "physical self", they do not consider blindness as a barrier in achieving the goals of life. The eminent blind personalities play as role models for them. However, the talented visually impaired children despite their visual impairment want to excel in different fields of life.

Status of the Talented Visually Impaired Children on "Leaning Styles"

Table 5 shows the status of the talented visually impaired children on "learning styles". A study of the table depicts that the group members varied to one another with regard to their preferred learning styles. The group's first, second, third and fourth preferred learning styles are "reflective observation', (understanding), "active experimentation" (doing), "abstract conceptualisation" (thinking) and "concrete experience" (feeling) respectively. It reveals that the group's most preferred learning style is "reflective observation" and the least preferred learning style is "concrete experience". It could be said that the talented visually impaired children learn best by using "reflective observation" learning style.

Table 5: Status of the Talented Visually Impaired Children on "Learning Styles"

Name of the variable	Sub areas of the variable	Mean score	Standard deviation	Variance	Minimum score	Maximum score
Learning styles	Active experimentation (AE)	30.33	4.35	18.96	23	38
	Concrete experience (CE)	25	5.37	28.9	17	35
	Abstract conceptualisation (AC)	27.16	6.17	˙38.14	19	38
	Reflective observation (RO)	37.1	4.12	16.99	30.00	44

An analysis of the responses made by the group with regard to its preferred learning style depicts that the talented visually impaired children during their learning phase focus on understanding the meaning of ideas and situations by carefully observing and impartially describing them. They seem to emphasise understanding as opposed to practical application, a concern with what is true or how things happen as opposed to what is practical. They tend to give importance on reflection as opposed to action. They appear to be good at looking at things from different perspectives and at appreciating different points of view. The talented visually impaired children rely on their own thoughts and feelings to form opinions. They value patience, impartiality and considered thoughtful judgement.

Status of the Visually Impaired Children on "Motivational Characteristics"

Table 6 shows the status of the talented visually impaired children on "motivational characteristic'. The group's AVAI score shows that the group possesses a moderate degree of "achievement motivation". This indicates that the talented visually impaired children are moderately achievement oriented. Though they lack visual sensory inputs, their future expectations are found positive and above average compared to the non-sighted peers.

Table 6: Status of the Talented Visually Impaired Children on "Motivational Characteristics"

Name of the variable	Sub areas of the variable	Mean score	Standard deviation	Variance	Minimum score	Maximum score
Motivational Characteristics	Achievement related motivation (AR)	13.25	2.137	4.567	10	17
	Task related motivation (TR)	6.75	1.764	3.112	4	9
	Unrelated motivation (UR)	1.83	1.46	2.15	00	4
	Total AVAI	**11.416**	–	–	7	17

A look at different dimensions of the motivational characteristics shows that the talented visually impaired children do possess higher "achievement related motivation" compared to "task related motivation". The group possesses a low unrelated motivation. This reflects that the talented visually impaired children do possess low anxiety.

Status of the Talented Speech & Hearing Impaired Children on "Teacher's Perception" and on "Perception of Self"

Table 7 shows the status of the talented speech and hearing impaired children on "teacher's perception" and on "perception of self". A study of the table reveals that teacher's perception of the group is found high. This reflects that teachers of the talented speech and hearing impaired children do possess high perception of talent aspect of this group of children. A look at the group's "perception of self" shows that the group possesses a low but positive "self". This reflects that the talented speech and hearing impaired children possess low perception of their strengths, abilities, worth, desires, goals and aspirations of life as a whole. A look at different dimensions of self reveals that the group possesses higher "academic self" than the group's "social self". This indicates that the talented speech and hearing impaired children are academic oriented. The group's physical self is found low. This shows that the talented speech and hearing impaired children possess low perception of their physical abilities.

Table 7: Status of the Talented Speech and Hearing Impaired Children on "Teacher's Perception" and on "Perception of Self".

Name of the variables	Sub areas of the variable	Mean score	Standard deviation	Variance	Minimum score	Maximum score
Teacher's perception	—	147.66	10.08	101.69	134	169
Perception of self	Academic Self (A.S.)	52.416	5.66	32.08	42	59
	Social Self (S.S.)	48.416	4.122	16.99	42	54
	Physical Self (P.S.)	13.00	1.348	1.817	10	15
	Total Self	**113.75**	**9.677**	**93.644**	**101**	**126**

An analysis of the responses made by the group reveals that the talented speech and hearing impaired children appear to be dedicated and sincere towards their academic work. They regularly attend their classes. They possess a highly developed sense of sincerity and punctuality. Compared to their peers these children do possess better understanding and grasping abilities. In the school they remain themselves busy both in academic and non-academic activities. Besides studies, they take part in games and sports, do drawing and painting work, successfully attend craft classes, and during the leasure hour they engage themselves in reading, writing and in doing other study related works. They never like a monotonous routine work. In their academic work they appear to be more achievement oriented.

A look at the social characteristics of the group reveals that the talented speech and hearing impaired children are not advanced in taking part in cultural activities and in social gatherings. They have limited friend circle. They do not find it easy in making friends with their hearing peers. They want to share their sorrows and joys among themselves only. They are found adventurous though they lack the ability to hear and speak. These children possess indifferent attitude towards leadership traits. They want to be loved and cared by everybody and appreciate the principle of equality.

A glance at "physical self" perception of the group reflects that the group possesses a low physical self. This indicates that the talented speech and hearing impaired children perceive their abilities, strength and communicating ability at a mild rate. They face difficulties in getting their things accomplished. This might be because of the fact that they lack hearing and communicating ability. They possess low future expectations.

Status of the Talented Speech and Hearing Impaired Children on "Learning Styles"

Table 8 shows the status of the talented speech and hearing impaired children on "learning styles". A study of this table reveals that the group members vary with regard to their preferred learning styles. So far as the group's learning style is concerned, the group shows more or less equal preferences for two learning styles, namely, "active experimentation" and "reflective observation". The other two learning styles, namely, "concrete experience" and "abstract conceptualisation" appear as third and fourth preferred learning styles of the group. This indicates that the talented speech and hearing impaired children possess two most preferred learning styles which are "active experimentation" and "reflective observation". The group's least preferred learning style is "abstract conceptualisation".

Table 8: Status of the Talented Speech and Hearing Impaired Children on "Learning Styles"

Name of the variable	Sub areas of the variable	Mean score	Standard deviation	Variance	Minimum score	Maximum score
Learning styles	Active experimentation (AE)	37	4.805	23.088	30	45
	Concrete experience (CE)	25	2.81	7.907	20	29
	Abstract conceptualisation (AC)	20.5	5.418	29.35	15	33
	Reflective observation (RO)	36.916	3.23	10.45	32	44

An analysis of responses made by the group reveals that the talented speech and hearing impaired children at their learning phase rely on "observation" as well as on "doing" depending on the nature of the learning task. It varies from one learning situation to another. In some learning situations they understand the meaning of ideas and concepts by carefully observing and describing them. In such situations they emphasise on understanding as opposed to practical application. In some other learning situations they emphasise on practical applications. In such cases they are willing to take some risk to achieve their learning objectives. They like to rely on their own thoughts and feelings to form opinions. They tend to be result oriented and are prone to see the learning outcomes.

Status of the Talented Speech and Hearing Impaired Children on "Motivational Characteristics"

Table 9 shows the status of the talented speech and hearing impaired children on "motivational characteristics". A study of this

Table 9: Status of the Talented Speech and Hearing Impaired Children on "Motivational Characteristics"

Name of the variable	Sub areas of the variable	Mean score	Standard deviation	Variance	Minimum score	Maximum score
Motivational Characteristics	Achievement related motivation (A.R.)	10.916	0.9	0.81	10	12
	Task Related motivation (T.R.)	7.25	1.138	1.295	5	9
	Unrelated motivation (U.R.)	3.83	1.403	1.968	2	7
	Total AVAI	**7.083**	–	–	**3**	**10**

table reveals that the group possesses a low "achievement motivation". This indicates that the talented speech and hearing impaired children have low "achievement motivation". Among the three facets of "motivational characteristics" the group's achievement related motivation compared to "task related motivation" is found high. The group also possesses low level of anxiety. This implies that the talented speech and hearing impaired children are not quite sure about their future success.

Status study of the three groups of talented exceptional children concludes the following:

1. Teachers of the talented orthopaedically impaired, talented visually impaired and talented speech and hearing impaired children show high ratings with regard to talent aspect of these children. Above average academic performance and overall achievement of these children were considered as talent indicator by their teachers.

3. "Perception of self" of each of the three categories of talented exceptional children is found low though positive. Among the three faces of self each of the three groups possesses high

"academic self" compared to "social self". The "physical self" of the talented orthopaedically impaired, talented visually impaired, and talented speech and hearing impaired children is found low.

3. The three groups vary with regard to their preferred learning styles. The predominant learning style(s) of the talented orthopaedically impaired children is "active experimentation" (doing); while it is "reflective observation" in case of the talented visually impaired children. The learning styles, namely, "active experimentation" and "reflective observation" are equally preferred by the talented speech and hearing impaired children.

4. The talented visually impaired children possess moderate degree of achievement motivation and the talented orthopaedically impaired and the talented speech and hearing impaired children possess low achievement motivation.

Statistical Comparison Section

This section deals with comparison between each of the three categories of talented exceptional children on different variables, namely, "teacher's perception", "perception of self", "learning styles" and "motivational characteristics". This section is divided into three subsections:

1. Comparison between talented orthopaedically impaired children and talented visually impaired children on "teacher's perception", "perception of self", "learning styles", and on "motivational characteristics".
2. Comparison between talented orthopaedically impaired children and talented speech and hearing impaired children on "teacher's perception', "perception of self", "learning styles" and on "motivational characteristics".
3. Comparison between talented visually impaired children and talented speech and hearing impaired children on "teacher's perception", "perception of self", "learning styles" and on "motivational characteristics".

Comparison Between Talented Orthopaedically Impaired Children and Talented Visually Impaired Children on "Teacher's Perception", "Perception of Self", "Learning Styles", and on "Motivational Characteristics".

Table 10 shows the statistical comparison between the talented orthopaedically impaired and talented visually impaired children on different variables. A study of this table reveals that the two groups differed significantly on variables like "teacher's perception", "perception of self", "active experimentation" learning style, and on "achievement motivation". The two groups did not differ significantly on "social self", "physical self", "concrete experience", "abstract conceptualisation' and "reflective observation", learning styles and on "task related motivation".

A significant difference between the two groups on "teacher's perception" shows that the talent aspect of the orthopaedically impaired children has been better perceived compared to that of the talented visually impaired children. An analysis of the responses made by the teachers reveals that the talented visually impaired children are poor in self expression despite the fact that they possess good academic performance. As reported by the teachers, these children appear to be gloomy and are not advanced in social traits and the teachers usually give excuses to them in many occasions. Teachers also undermine their abilities because of their poor self expression. In contrast talented orthopaedically impaired children are comparatively better than the talented visually impaired children in self expression.

On "perception of self", the difference between the two groups is found to be significant at 0.05 level. This reflects that the talented orthopaedically impaired children possess high positive perception of self than the talented visually impaired children. The talented orthopaedically impaired children seem to be more risk oriented, advanced in socialisation, and are quite sure about their abilities compared to the talented visually impaired children. In contrast the talented visually impaired children appear to perceive their worth and abilities at a low rate. It might be because of lack of vision. The difference between the two groups on "academic self" is found to be significant at 0.01 level. Such a significant difference reflects that the talented orthopaedically

Table 10: Statistical Comparison between Talented Orthopedically Impaired And Visually Impaired Children On Different Variables

Name of the variables	M_1	M_2	S.D.	S_{ED}	$M_1 - M_2$	't' Value	Level of Significance
Teacher's perception	153.5	141.66	10.017	4.037	11.334	2.89	0.01
Academic self	57.25	53.166	3.534	1.442	4.084	2.83	0.01
Social self	51.666	49.166	3.619	1.477	2.5	1.69	N.S.
Physical self	13.166	14.25	2.099	0.857	−0.584	−0.68	N.S.
Perception of self (Total)	122.583	116.166	7.015	2.862	6.417	2.34	0.05
Active Experimentation ($L.S._1$)	37.166	30.33	4.693	1.915	6.833	3.57	0.01
Concrete Experience ($L.S._2$)	26.00	25.00	4.99	2.039	1.00	0.49	N.S.
Abstract conceptualisation ($L.S._3$)	24.75	27.166	6.476	2.642	−2.416	−0.91	N.S.
Reflective Observation ($L.S._4$)	33.5	37.083	5.259	2.145	−3.583	−1.67	N.S.
Achievement Related Motivation	10.66	13.25	1.95	0.797	−2.584	−3.24	0.01
Task Related motivation	6.33	6.75	1.525	0.622	−0.417	−0.67	N.S.
Unrelated motivation	5.00	1.833	1.631	0.665	3.167	4.76	0.01

M_1 : Mean of the talented orthopedically impaired children.

M_2 : Mean of the talented visually impaired children.

N.S. : Non Significant

impaired children possess higher "academic self" than the talented visually impaired children. It also reflects that the previous group is more academic oriented than the latter. On "social self" and "physical self" no significant differences were found between the two groups. This indicates that both talented orthopaedically impaired and visually impaired children perceive their physical self and social self in the same manner. It could be said that neither of the group is superior to one another in perceiving their physical abilities and social traits.

A study of the group differences on "learning styles" shows that both the groups only differ significantly at 0.01 level on "active experimentation learning style". This reflects that the talented orthopaedically impaired children display more positive attitudes towards "active experimentation" learning style, compared to the talented visually impaired children. This shows that the talented orthopaedically impaired children compared to the talented visually impaired children are good at getting things accomplished, willing to take some risk to achieve their objectives, influencing on the environment around them and like to see the learning results. On three other learning styles, namely, concrete experience, abstract conceptualisation, and reflective observation no significant differences among the groups are reported. This shows that these three learning styles were more or less equally preferred by both the talented orthopaedically impaired and talented visually impaired children.

An analysis of the group differences on motivational characteristics reveals that both the groups differ significantly at 0.01 level on "achievement motivation". This shows that the talented visually impaired children possess high achievement motivation compared to the talented orthopaedically impaired children. This indicates that the previous group possesses more optimistic view of life and more drive to achieve than the latter. On task related motivation the two groups do not show any significant difference. This reflects that both the talented orthopaedically impaired and the talented visually impaired children possess the same level of drive to complete the assigned task.

In conclusion, it could be said that the talented orthopaedically impaired children, though, possess higher perception of self than the talented visually impaired children, the previous group displays less "achievement motivation" than the latter. The two groups show more or less same order of preferences for "concrete experience", "abstract conceptualisation", and "reflective observation" but not for "active experimentation" so far as their learning styles are concerned.

Comparison between Talented Orthopaedically Impaired and Speech and Hearing Impaired Children on Different Variables

Table 11 shows the comparative study between the talented orthopaedically impaired and the talented speech and hearing impaired children on different variables. A study of this table shows that the two groups differ significantly on "academic self", "social self" and on "abstract conceptualisation" learning style. Both the groups do not differ significantly on "teacher's perception", "physical self", "achievement motivation", "task motivation' and on three other learning styles, namely, "active experimentation", "concrete experience", and "reflective observation".

A detailed study of the table reveals that the talented orthopaedically impaired and talented speech and hearing impaired children do not differ significantly on teacher's perception. This reflects that the talent aspect of both the two groups are equally perceived by their concerned teachers.

An analysis of the group differences on various "self" aspects shows that the talented orthopaedically impaired and talented speech and hearing impaired children differ significantly at 0.05 level on "academic self". This reveals that the talented orthopaedically impaired children possess high "academic self" than the talented speech and hearing impaired children. Or in other words it could be said that the previous group seems to be more prone to attain academic success compared to the latter. On "social self" the difference between the two groups is found to be significant at 0.05 level. This reflects that the talented orthopaedically impaired children possess better perception of their social self than the talented speech and hearing impaired children. It indicates that the talented orthopaedically impaired children compared to the talented speech and hearing impaired

Table 11: Statistical Comparison between Talented Orthopedically Impaired and Speech and Hearing Impaired Children on Different Variables

Name of the variables	M_1	M_2	S.D.	S_{ED}	M_1-M_2	't' Value	Level of significance
Teacher's perception	153.5	147.66	10.401	4.243	5.834	1.37	N.S.
Academic self	57.25	52.146	4.854	1.98	5.104	2.58	0.05
Social self	51.66	48.146	3.574	1.458	3.52	2.41	0.05
Physical self	13.66	13.0	1.553	0.634	0.666	1.05	N.S.
Perception of self (Total)	122.58	113.75	8.129	3.317	8.833	2.66	0.05
Active Experimentation ($L.S_1$)	37.166	37	4.927	2.01	0.166	0.08	N.S.
Concrete Experience ($L.S._2$)	26.00	25.5	3.679	1.501	0.5	0.33	N.S.
Abstract conceptualisation ($L.S._3$)	24.75	20.5	4.001	1.632	4.25	2.6	0.05
Reflective observation ($L.S._4$)	33.5	36.916	4.908	2.003	–3.416	–1.71	N.S.
Achievement related motivation	10.66	10.916	1.328	0.542	–0.25	–0.46	N.S.
Task related motivation	6.33	7.25	1.195	0.471	–0.917	–1.95	N.S.
Unrelated motivation	5.00	3.833	1.6	0.652	1.167	1.79	N.S.

M_1 : Mean of the talented orthopedically impaired children.

M_2 : Mean of the talented speech and hearing impaired children.

N.S. : Non-significant.

children are more advanced so far as their social traits are concerned.

A comparative study between the two groups on their preferred learning styles reveals that the two groups do not differ significantly on three learning styles, namely, "active experimentation", "concrete experience" and reflective observation". This shows that both the groups show more or less same order of preferences for these three learning styles. However, the two groups differ significantly on "abstract conceptualisation" learning style at 0.05 level. This shows that the talented orthopaedically impaired children compared to the talented speech and hearing impaired children show a stronger preference for "abstract conceptualisation" as preferred learning style. It could be said that the talented orthopaedically impaired children are markedly superior to the talented speech and hearing impaired children in learning new tasks and concepts by using logical thinking as opposed to feeling. The previous group is good at systematic planning, manipulation of abstract symbols and quantitative analysis. The talented orthopaedically impaired children compared to the talented speech and hearing impaired children are markedly superior in value precision, analysing ideas in aesthetic quality and in conceptual system.

An analysis of the motivational characteristics of the two groups reveals that both the groups do not differ significantly on "achievement motivation" and on task related motivation. This reflects that though, the talented orthopaedically impaired children as reported earlier possess higher perception of self than the talented speech and hearing impaired children, the two groups display same degree of "achievement motivation". Their future expectations are more or less low and both the groups do not possess high degree of drive to success.

In conclusion it could be said that both the groups are equally rated by their concerned teachers so far as their talent aspect is concerned. The talented orthopaedically impaired children seem to possess high academic self and social self than the talented speech and hearing impaired children. The talented orthopaedically impaired children are superior to the talented speech and hearing impaired children on logical thinking. Though the talented orthopaedically impaired children do possess high academic and social self than the talented speech and hearing impaired children, the two groups do possess same level of achievement motivation.

Statistitical Comparison between Talented Visually Impaired and Talented Speech and Hearing Impaired Children on Different Variables

Table 12 shows the comparison between the talented visually impaired and talented speech and hearing impaired children on different variables. A study of this table reveals that the two groups differ significantly on learning styles, namely, "active experimentation' and "abstract conceptualisation', and on "achievement motivation". The two groups do not differ significantly on "teacher's perception", "academic self", "social self", "physical self", "concrete experience" and on "reflective observation' learning styles and on "task related motivation".

An analysis of this table reveals that the two groups do not differ significantly on their teacher's perception. This reflects that the talent aspect of both the talented visually impaired and talented speech and hearing impaired children are equally perceived by their concerned teachers.

Both the talented visually impaired children and the talented speech and hearing impaired children show no significant differences on "academic self", "social self", and on "physical self". This reflects that neither of the group is superior to other academically, socially and physically so far as their perception of self is concerned.

A comparative study between the two groups on their preferred learning styles reveals that the two groups differ significantly on "active experimentation' at 0.01 level and on "abstract conceptualisation" at 0.05 level. This shows that both the groups differ in choosing "active experimentation" and "abstract conceptualisation" as their preferred learning styles. The talented speech and hearing impaired children are found superior to the talented visually impaired children on "active experimentation" domain and just the vice versa on "abstract conceptualisation" domain. The learning task involving practical

Table 12: Statistical Comparison between Talented Visually Impaired and Talented Speech and Hearing Impaired Children on Different Variables

Name of the variables	M_1	M_2	S.D.	S_{ED}	M_1-M_2	't' Value	Level of significance
Teaher's perception	141.66	147.66	10.154	4.143	-6.00	-1.45	N.S.
Academic self	53.166	52.146	4.892	1.996	1.02	0.51	N.S.
Social self	49.166	48.146	4.344	1.772	1.02	0.58	N.S.
Physical self	14.25	13.00	1.995	0.814	1.25	1.54	N.S.
Perception of self (Total)	116.166	113.75	9.235	3.768	2.416	0.64	N.S.
Active experimentation (L.S.$_1$)	30.33	37.00	4.789	1.954	-6.667	-3.41	0.01
Concrete experience (L.S.$_2$)	25.00	25.5	4.48	1.828	-0.5	-0.27	N.S.
Abstract conceptualisation (L.S.$_3$)	27.166	20.5	6.067	2.475	6.66	2.69	0.05
Reflective observation (L.S.$_4$)	37.08	36.916	3.868	1.578	0.167	0.11	N.S.
Achievement related motivation	13.25	10.916	1.713	0.699	2.334	3.34	0.01
Task related motivation	6.75	7.25	1.55	0.633	-0.5	-0.79	N.S.
Unrelated motivation	1.833	3.833	1.499	0.611	-2.00	-3.27	0.01

M_1 : Mean of the talented visually impaired children.

M_2 : Mean of the talented speech and hearing impaired children.

N.S. : Non-Significant.

activities as opposed to reflective understanding is found to be mastered by the talented speech and hearing impaired children and the learning task involving logical thinking as opposed to feeling is found to be mastered by the talented visually impaired children easily. However, the two groups show similar preferences for the two other learning styles, namely, "concrete experience" and "reflective observation".

An analysis of the "motivational characteristics" of the talented visually impaired and talented speech and hearing impaired children depicts that the two groups differ significantly at 0.01 level on "achievement motivation". This reflects that the talented visually impaired children do possess high achievement motivation than the talented speech and hearing impaired children. Despite the fact that the previous group lacks visual sensory inputs, still compared to the latter one possesses better positive attitudes towards attainment of success in life. Lack of oral communication ability (language) makes the talented speech and hearing impaired children to possess low drive towards success. However, the two groups do not differ significantly on task related motivation. This shows that both the talented visually impaired and the talented speech and hearing impaired children possess more or less the same degree of drive to complete the assigned task.

To conclude, it could be said that the talented visually impaired and talented speech and hearing impaired children do not differ on their "teacher's perception" as well as on "perception of self". Both the groups differ significantly on "active experimentation" and "abstract conceptualisation" so far as their learning styles are concerned. The talented visually impaired children are more achievement oriented than the talented speech and hearing impaired children.

Correlational Studies

This section attempts to show intercorrelations among different pairs of variables considered for the study like, "teacher's perception" with "perception" of self"; "teacher's perception" with "learning styles"; "teacher's perception" with "motivational characteristics"; perception of self" with "learning styles"; "perception of self" with "motivational characteristics" and "learning styles" with "motivational characteristics" of the talented exceptional children. The correlation coefficients are shown in separate matrixes for each of the three categories of talented exceptional children. Each box of the matrix shows two values, the upper one stands for correlation coefficient while the lower one indicates the level of significance.

This section has been divided into the following three sub-sections.

1. Inter-correlations among different variables—Talented orthopaedically impaired children.
2. Inter-correlations among different variables—Talented visually impaired children.
3. Inter-correlations among different variables—Talented speech and hearing impaired children.

Inter-Correlations among Different Variables—Talented Orthopaedically Impaired Children

Table 13 shows the intercorrelations among different pairs of variables of the talented orthopaedically impaired children. A thorough study of this table reveals that "teacher's perception" of the group correlated positively with the group's "perception of self" (academic self and physical self), and three learning styles, namely, "active experimentation", "concrete experience", and "reflective observation". The "teacher's perception" of the group correlated negatively with "concrete experience" learning style, "achievement motivation" and "task related motivation'. "Perception of self" of the group correlated positively with the group's most preferred learning style i.e. "active experimentation" and "reflective observation" and correlated negatively with the group's least preferred learning styles i.e., "concrete experience" and "abstract conceptualisation'. The group's most preferred learning style correlated positively with the group's "achievement motivation".

An analysis of correlation coefficients of the group's "teacher's perception" with other variables reveals that the group's "academic self". "physical self", and most preferred learning styles i.e., "active experimentation' and "reflective observation" possess positive affect on the group's "teacher's perception". It could then be said that teacher's perception of talent aspect of the orthopaedically impaired children is dependent on the group's academic performance, physical abilities and preferred learning

Table 13: Intercorrelations among Different Variables Group: Talented Orthopedically Impaired Children (Correlation Matrix)

Variables	Ac.S.	So.S.	Ph.S.	Sel.P.(t)	L.S.$_1$	L.S.$_2$	L.S.$_3$	L.S.$_4$	Ach. Mot.	Ta. Mot
Tea Per	0.096	–0.182	0.241	0.046	0.312	–0.223	0.177	0.092	–0.089	–0.551
	0.76	0.57	0.45	0.88	0.32	0.43	0.58	0.77	0.78	0.06
Ac.S.	–	0.161	0.051	0.729	0.398	–0.583	–0.124	–0.016	0.210	0.432
	–	0.61	0.87	0.007	0.20	0.04	0.70	0.95	0.51	0.16
So.S.	–	–	0.504	0.740	0.555	–0.323	–0.599	0.259	0.384	–0.022
			0.09	0.005	0.06	0.30	0.03	0.41	0.21	0.94
Ph.S.	–	–	–	0.583	0.604	–0.328	–0.253	–0.096	–0.084	–0.192
				0.04	0.03	0.29	0.42	0.76	0.79	0.54
Sel.P.(t)	–	–	–	–	0.70	–0.628	–0.446	0.085	0.292	0.204
					0.01	0.02	0.14	0.79	0.35	0.52
L.S$_1$	–	–	–	–	–	–	–	–	0.008	–0.04
									0.97	0.38
L.S$_2$	–	–	–	–	–	–	–	–	–0.07	0.47
									0.82	0.11
L.S$_3$	–	–	–	–	–	–	–	–	–0.121	0.06
									0.70	0.83
L.S$_4$	–	–	–	–	–	–	–	–	0.1005	–0.117
									0.75	0.71

N.B. : Correlation coefficients/PROB>IRI Under HO: RHO = O/N=12

Tea. Per. Teacher's perception
Ac.S. Academic self
So.S. Social self
Ph. S. Physical self
Sel.P.(t) Perception of self (total)
L.S.$_1$ Active experimentation learning style
L.S.$_2$ Concrete Experience learning style
L.S.$_3$ Abstract conceptualisation learning style
L.S.$_4$ Reflective observation learning style
Ach. Mot. Achievement motivation
Ta. Mot. Task motivation

styles. An analysis of the responses made by the teachers reveals that "for talent identification, teachers had focused on the overall academic achievement and performance in co-curricular activities of the talented orthopaedically impaired children. Since there exists negative relationships between teacher's perception and motivational characteristics of the group, it could be said that the motivational traits of the talented orthopaedically impaired children do not affect their teacher's perception. Thus, the study reveals that physical self and the group's two most preferred learning styles appear to affect the teacher's perception of the talented orthopaedically impaired children.

An analysis of coefficients of correlation of perception of self with group's preferred learning styles and motivational characteristics reveals that a significant positive correlation is found between perception of self and "active experimentation" learning style. This reflects that there exists a significant positive substantial relationship between perception of self and most preferred learning style of the talented orthopaedically impaired children. The relationship between perception of self and motivational characteristics of the group is not found substantial. Group's perception of self possesses negative relationship with the group's least preferred learning style. Low positive relationship exists between group's academic self and group's most preferred learning style. Social self possesses substantial positive relationship with the group's most preferred learning style and moderate positive relationship with "achievement motivation". A significant positive correlation exists among the group's physical self and most preferred learning style. This indicates that there exists positive substantial relationship between the physical self and most preferred learning style of the talented orthopaedically impaired children. No substantial relationship is found among the group's preferred learning styles and motivational characteristics.

Inter-correlations among Different Variables: Talented Visually Impaired Children

Table 14 shows the correlation coefficients of the talented visually impaired children among various variables as taken in the present study. A detailed study of the table shows that the

Table 14: Inter-correlations among Different Variables
Group: Talented Visually Impaired Children (Correlation Matrix)

Variables	Ac.S.	So.S.	Ph.S.	Sel.P.(t)	$L.S._1$	$L.S._2$	$L.S._3$	$L.S._4$	Ach. Mot.	Ta. Mot
Tea. Per.	−0.6555	0.1638	0.353	−0.115	−0.332	0.045	0.368	−0.266	0.787	−0.650
	0.02	0.61	0.259	0.72	0.29	0.88	0.23	0.40	0.002	0.02
Ac.S.	–	−0.034	−0.062	0.256	0.409	0.148	−0.426	0.185	−0.465	0.293
		0.91	0.084	0.42	0.18	0.64	0.16	0.56	0.12	0.35
So.S.	–	–	0.356	0.590	−0.092	−0.536	0.171	0.556	−0.035	−0.632
			0.25	0.04	0.77	0.07	0.59	0.06	0.91	0.02
Ph.S.	–	–	–	0.414	0.134	−0.173	0.211	−0.125	0.277	−0.512
				0.18	0.67	0.59	0.51	0.69	0.38	0.08
Sel.P.(t)	–	–	–	–	0.446	−0.613	0.014	0.264	−0.475	−0.016
					0.14	0.03	0.96	0.40	0.11	0.96
$L.S_1$	–	–	–	–	–	–	–	–	−0.205	0.355
									0.52	0.25
$L.S._2$	–	–	–	–	–	–	–	–	0.293	−0.048
									0.35	0.88
$L.S._3$	–	–	–	–	–	–	–	–	0.058	−0.296
									0.85	0.35
$L.S._4$	–	–	–	–	–	–	–	–	−0.199	−0.009
									0.53	0.97

N.B. : Correlation Coefficients/Prob>IRI under HO: RHO = O/N=12

Tea. Per. Teacher's perception
Ph. S Physical self
$L.S._1$ Active experimentation learning style
$L.S._3$ Abstract conceptualisation learning style
Ach. Mot. Achievement motivation
Ac.S. Academic self
Sel.P.(t) Perception of self (Total)
$L.S._2$ Concrete expeirnece learning style
$L.S._4$ Reflective observation learning style
Ta. Mot. Task Motivtion
So.S. Social self

teacher's perception of the group correlated positively with the group's social self, physical self, two learning styles, namely, concrete experience and abstract conceptualisation and with "achievement motivation". And it correlated negatively with the group's academic self, two learning styles, namely, "active experimentation" and "reflective observation" and with task related motivation. This indicates that teacher's perception of the talented visually impaired children shows relationship with the group's social self, physical self, and with the group's least preferred learning styles, namely, "concrete experience" and "abstract conceptualsiation", and with their "achievement motivation". And it shows no relationship with their academic self, most preferred learning styles, namely, "reflective observation" and "active experimentation", and with "task related motivation". In other words it could be explained that teachers of the talented visually impaired children perceived the talent aspect of these children by taking into account their social traits, physical abilities, "achievement motivation", logical thinking ability, sense of aesthetic quality, intuitive decision making ability and open-mindedness. However, the academic self and the most preferred learning style i.e., reflective observation, of the talented visually impaired children do not substantially contribute so far as the teacher's perception of these children is concerned. It reflects that the teachers of the talented visually impaired children either fail to understand them or pay little attention for the nurturance of their talents.

A study of the correlation coefficients of perception of self with learning styles and motivational characteristics of the talented visually impaired children shows that it correlates positively with three of the learning styles, namely, "active experimentation", "abstract conceptualisation", and "reflective observation". And it correlates negatively with "concrete experience" learning style, "achievement motivation" and "task related motivation" of the group. It indicates that the group's perception of self shows positive relationship with its preferred learning style and possesses no relationship with motivational characteristics. In other words, it could be said that the perception of self abilities and worth of the talented visually impaired children influence their approaches they do put for learning new texts and concepts.

However, their future achievement motivation does not appear to be affected by their perception of won abilities, worth and aspirations. The group's "academic self" appears to correlate positively with three of the learning styles, namely, active experimentation, concrete experience, and "reflective observation and with "task related motivation". It indicates that the academic self of the talented visually impaired children does effect their preferred learning styles and task related motivation. They appear to be more academic oriented, sincere and punctual in learning and in completing the assigned task. Their academic perception of self abilities however does not affect their future goals of life i.e. achievement motivation. The social self also shows positive relationship with the group's most preferred learning style i.e. reflective observation and negative relationship with their motivational characteristics. The group's physical self shows positive correlation with two of the learning styles, namely, active experimentation and abstract conceptualisation and with achievement motivation. It indicates that perception of physical abilities of the group has positive effect on the group's achievement motivation. In other words, it could be said that the talented visually impaired children are quite sure about their success and achievement of life's goals despite the fact that they lack vision. This kind of success oriented feeling also has been manifested in the physical self-perception of the talented visually impaired children.

A study of the correlation coefficients of the group's most preferred learning style i.e. reflective observation with group's motivational characteristics shows that it correlates negatively both with "achievement motivation" and "task related motivation". This indicates that the motivational characteristics of the talented visually impaired children are not affected by their preferred styles of learning.

Inter-correlations among Different Variables: Talented Speech and Hearing Impaired Children

Table 15 shows the correlation coefficients among different pairs of variables of the talented speech and hearing impaired children. A thorough study of this table shows that teacher's

Table 15. Inter-correlations among Different Variables
Group: Talented Speech & Hearing Impaired Children (Correlation Matrix)

Variables	Ac.S.	So.S.	Ph.S.	Sel.P.(t)	L.S.$_1$	L.S.$_2$	L.S.$_3$	L.S.$_4$	Ach. Mot.	Ta. Mot
Tea. Per.	–0.136 0.67	–0.377 0.22	–0.261 0.41	0.265 0.40	–0.566 0.05	0.397 0.20	0.266 0.40	0.060 0.85	–0.063 0.84	–0.293 0.35
Ac.S.	–	0.782 0.002	0.357 0.25	0.966 0.0001	0.417 0.17	0.353 0.26	–0.206 0.52	–0.609 0.03	–0.224 0.48	0.349 0.26
So.S.	–	–	0.114 0.72	0.896 0.0001	0.229 0.47	0.027 0.93	0.205 0.52	–0.754 0.004	0.010 0.97	0.576 0.04
Ph.S.	–	–	–	0.397 0.20	0.519 0.08	0.239 0.45	–0.510 0.09	–0.062 0.84	–0.374 0.23	0.118 0.71
Sel.P.(t)	–	–	–	–	0.408 0.18	0.245 0.44	–0.094 0.77	–0.689 0.01	–0.169 0.59	0.468 0.12
L.S$_1$	–	–	–	–	–	–	–	–	–0.210 0.51	0.249 0.43
L.S$_2$	–	–	–	–	–	–	–	–	–0.449 0.14	0.269 0.39
L.S$_3$	–	–	–	–	–	–	–	–	0.326 0.30	–0.140 0.66
L.S$_4$	–	–	–	–	–	–	–	–	0.154 0.63	–0.364 0.24

N.B. : Correlation Coefficients/Prob>IRI under HO: RHO = O/N=12

Tea. Per. Teacher's perception
Ph. S. Physical self
L.S.$_1$ Active experimentation learning style
L.S.$_3$ Abstract conceptualisation learning style
Ach. Mot. Achievement motivation
Ac.S. Academic self
Sel.P.(t) Perception of self (Total)
L.S.$_2$ Concrete experience learning style
L.S.$_4$ Reflective observation learning style
Ta. Mot. Task motivtion
So.S. Social self

perception of the group correlates positively with three learning styles, namely, "concrete experience", "abstract conceptualisation" and "reflective observation". And correlates negatively with "perception of self" (academic self, social self, and physical self), "active experimentation" learning style, "achievement motivation', and "task related motivation". This indicates that "teacher's perception" of the group shows positive relationship with the group's preferred learning styles and negative relationship with "motivational characteristics" and with "perception of self". It reflects that teacher's perception of the talented speech and hearing impaired children is dependent on the preferred learning styles of these children. The learning characteristics, on the basis of which the teachers perceived the talent aspect of this group of children could be listed as: intuitive thinking ability, aristic approach, reflective understanding, patience, thoughtful judgements, and logical thinking ability. However, the group's achievement motivation and task completing ability do not appear to affect the teacher's perception.

A study of correlation coefficients of "perception of self" with "learning styles" and motivational characteristics reveals that it correlates positively with group's two learning styles, namely, "active experimentation", "concrete experience". It also correlates positively with "task related motivation" of the group. It correlates negatively with two other learning styles, namely, "abstract conceptualistion", and "reflective observation" and also with the group's "achievement motivation'. It reflects that the group's "perception of self" positively affects the group's preferred learning styles and task related motivation but not the achievement motivation. It could be explained that the approaches the talented speech and hearing impaired children put for learning are dependent on their perception of academic abilities, social traits and physical characteristics (body image). However, the perception of self abilities of the talented speech and hearing impaired children does not affect their achievement.

The correlates of achievement motivation are found to be "reflective observation" and "abstract conceptualisation" learning styles. The group's most preferred learning style i.e. "active experimentation" is negatively correlated with the group's achievement motivation. It shows that the group's most preferred learning style does not affect the group's achievement motivation. However, the group's most preferred learning style i.e. "active experimentation" has positive affect on the group's task completion motivation. This indicates that the talented speech and hearing impaired children are more prone to complete the assigned learning task and employ learning approaches accordingly.

Regression Equations and Their Analysis

The correctional studies could show the inter-correlations among pairs of variables as taken in the present study. However, to find out the effect of each independent affective variables on the dependent variables both separately and conjointly, the regression equations were calculated. Besides, the regression equations helped the researcher to know about the strength of predictability of teacher's perception and "perception of self" on the basis of independent variables dealt in this study. Simple, double and multiple regression equations were calculated for the talented "orthopaedically impaired", "visually impaired" and "speech and hearing impaired" children separately. Presentation of this section follows the below given sequence:

1. Simple, double and multiple regression equations, and their analysis-talented orthopaedically impaired children.
2. Simple, double and multiple regression equations and their analysis-talented visually impaired children.
3. Simple, double and multiple regression equations and their analysis-talented speech and hearing impaired children.

Simple, Double and Multiple Regression Equations, and Their Analysis-Talented Orthopaedically Impaired Children

This subsection deals with simple, double and multiple regression equations and their analysis among different variables of the talented orthopaedically impaired children. Calculation of regression equations are done as follows:

1. Simple, double and multiple regression equations, were calculated between "teacher's perception", "perception of self", "learning styles", "achievement motivation" and "task related motivation", where "teacher's perception" was considered as dependent variable and others as independent variables.

2. Simple, double and multiple regression equations were calculated between "perception of self", "learning styles", "achievement motivation" and "task related motivation", where "perception of self" was considered as dependent variables and others as independent ones.

The tables 16 to 21 represent the single double and multiple regression equations and their analysis between "teacher's perception", "perception of self", "learning styles", and "motivational characteristics" of the talented orthopaedically impaired children where "teacher's perception" has been considered as dependent variable. Referring to Table 16, it was found that among all the single variables considered as independent ones the equation carrying "task related motivation" possesses high R-value which is significant at 0.06 level. All other equations carry low R-values. It indicates that "teacher's perception" of the group could be predicted only on the basis of group's "task related motivation". Or in other words it could be explained that among all the single variables "task related motivation" could be considered as the best one for the purpose of prediction of "teacher's perception" of the talented orthopaedically impaired children.

Table 17 shows the double regression equations each one carrying three variables between the "teacher's perception", "perception of self', "learning styles", and "motivational characteristics" of the talented orthopaedically impaired children. In each equation two affective variables were taken for the purpose of prediction. A thorough study of the table depicts that equation numbers 2, 3, 6, 8 and 14, carry high R-values while all other equations carry low R-values. However, among the above stated equations the R-value is found to be significant only in case of equation No. 4 carrying "concrete experience" and "task related motivation" as the pair of affective variables. Although "task related motivation" paired with either "active experimentation", "abstract conceptualisation" or with "reflective observation" as independent variables appear to possess high R-values; these values are found non-significant and henceforth could not be considered for the purpose of prediction. This indicates that among all the pairs of affective variables taken in table 17 for the purpose of prediction of "teacher's perception" of the group, "concrete

Table 16: Single Regression Equations: Group Talented Orthopedically Impaired Children Dependent Variable: Teacher's Perception

Sl. No.	Name of the variables	The equations	R-Value	F-Value	Prob>F
1.	Teach. Perc. Ach. Mot.	Tea. Perc. = 159.5–0.5625 Ach. Mot.	0.0889	0.080	0.78
2.	Teach. Perc.. Ta. Mot.	Tea. Perc. = 185.5–5.0526 Ta. Mot.	0.5515	4.322	0.06
3.	Teach. Perc., $L.S_1$	Teach. Perc. = 128.897 + 0.6619 $L.S_1$	0.3116	1.076	0.32
4.	Teach. Perc., $L.S._2$	Teach. Perc. = 167.338 – 0.5322 $L.S._2$	0.2227	0.522	0.48
5.	Teach. Perc., $L.S_{.3}$	Teach. Perc. = 146.561 + 0.2803 $L.S._3$	0.0315	0.325	0.58
6.	Teach. Perc., $L.S_4$	Teach. Perc., = 148.262 + 0.1563 $L.S_4$	0.0922	0.086	0.78
7.	Teach. Perc., Sel, Perc.	Teach. Perc. = 142.776 + 0.0874 Sel. Pec.	0.0469	0.022	0.88

Table 17: Double Regression Equations: Group: Talented orthopedically Impaired Children Dependent Variable—Teacher's Perception

Sl. No.	Name of the variables	The equation(s)	R-Value	F-Value	Prob>F
1.	Tea. Perc, L.S_1, Ach. Mot.	Tea. Perc. = 135.013 + 0.6635 L.S_1 – 0.5790 Ach. Mot.	0.3249	0.531	0.60
2.	Tea. Perc. L.S_1 Ta. Mot.	Tea. Perc. = 162.16 + 0.6062 L.S_1 – 4.925 Ta.Mot	0.6208	2.823	0.11
3.	Tea. Perc, L.S.$_2$ Ach. Mot.	Tea. Perc. = 174.904 – 0.5501 L.S_2 – 0.6656 Ach. Mot	0.2462	0.290	0.75
4.	Tea. Perc, L.S_2 Ta. Mot.	Tea. Perc. = 241.452 – 1.492 L.S_2 – 7.7619 Ta. Mot.	0.7787	6.929	0.01
5.	Tea. Perc, L.S_3 Ach. Mot.	Tea. Perc. = 151.498 + 0.2671 L.S.$_3$ – 0.4322 Ach. Mot.	0.19	1.169	0.84
6.	Tea. Perc, L.S_3. Ta. Mot.	Tea. Perc. = 177.908 + 0.3412 L.S.$_3$ – 5.1873 Ta.Mot.	0.5922	2.430	0.14
7.	Tea. Perc, L.S_4 Ach. Mot.	Tea. Perc. = 154.389 + 0.1732 L.S.$_4$ – 0.6274 Ach. Mot.	0.1353	0.084	0.92
8.	Tea. Perc, L.S_4 Ta. Mot.	Tea. Perc. = 183.698 + 0.048 L.S_4 – 5.022 Ta. Mot.	0.5523	1.975	0.19
9.	Tea. Perc, Sel. Perc, L.S.$_1$	Tea. Perc. = 189.19 – 0.6496 Sel. Perc. + 1.1825 L.S_1	0.3966	0.840	0.46
10.	Tea. Perc, Sel. Perc, L.S.$_2$	Tea. Perc. = 208.595 – 0.2876 Sel. Per. + 0.7627 L.S.$_2$	0.2528	0.307	0.74
11.	Tea. Perc, Sel. Perc, L.S.$_3$	Tea. Perc. = 107.741 + 0.2943 Sel. Per. + 0.3910 L.S_3	0.2265	0.243	0.78
12.	Tea. Perc, Sel. Perc, L.S.$_4$	Tea. Perc. = 139.465 + 0.0733 Sel. Per. + 0.1507 L.S_4	0.1005	0.046	0.95
13.	Tea. Perc, Sel. Perc, Ach. Mot.	Tea. Perc = 142.783 + 0.149 Sel. Perc. – 0.709 Ach. Mot.	0.1171	0.063	0.93
14.	Tea. Perc, Sel. Perc, Ta.Mot.	Tea. Perc = 149.253+0.3118 Sel. Per. – 5.3644 Ta.Mot	0.5751	2.24	0.16

experience learning style" and "task related motivation" are found to be effective ones. Here it could be said that "teacher's perception" of the talented orthopaedically impaired children could be predicted only on the basis of pair of variables, namely, "Concrete experience learning style" and "task related activation".

Table 18, shows the multiple regression equations and their analysis among "teacher's perception" and other variables as taken in the study of the talented orthopaedically impaired children. Among all the equations the first three equations carry high 'R' values which are also found significant. A look at these three equations reflects that the group of variables which could be considered conjointly for the purpose of prediction of "teacher's perception" of the group are "active experimentation" and "concrete experience" learning styles; "achievement motivation", "task related motivation" and "perception of self". In other words it could be said that prediction of "teacher's perception" of the talented orthopaedically impaired children could be made on the basis of the group's "perception of self", "learning styles" and "motivational characteristics" conjointly.

Tables 19, 20 and 21 show the single, double and multiple regression equations and their analysis of the talented orthopaedically impaired children among "perception of self", "learning styles" and "motivational characteristics (achievement motivation and task related motivation)" where "perception of self" has been considered as dependent variable. A thorough study of the table 19 reveals that among all the six equations as shown, only equation no. 3, carrying "perception of self" and "active experimentation" learning style, and equation no. 4, carrying "perception of self" and "concrete experience learning style" appear to possess high R-values which are found significant at 0.01 and 0.02 level respectively. The equations carrying "achievement motivation" and "task related motivation" do not possess significant R-values and these could not be used for the purpose of prediction. This indicates that among each of the four "learning styles", "achievement motivation", and "task related motivation", both "active experimentation" and "concrete experience" learning styles were found suitable single variabel(s) for the purpose of prediction of "perception of self" of the group. It could be then said that prediction of "perception of self" of the talented orthopaedically

Table 18: Multiple Regression Equations: Group: Talented Orthopedically Impaired Children Dependent Variable: Teacher's Perception

Sl. No.	Name of the variables	The equations	R-Value	F-Value	Prob>F
1.	Tea. Perc. $L.S_2$, Ach. Mot. Ta. Mot.	Tea Perc. = 282.334 – 1.7234 $L.S_2$ – 2.4772 Ach. Mot. 9.0947 Ta.Mot.	0.86189	7.71	0.009
2.	Tea. Perc. $L.S_1$ $L.S_2$, Ach. Mot. Ta.Mot.	Tea Perc. = 349.764 – 0.8232 $L.S_1$ – 2.5230 $L.S_2$ – 2.9194 Ach. Mot. – 10.8828 Ta.Mot.	0.9003	7.49	0.01
3.	Tea. Perc. Sel. Perc. $L.S_1$, $L.S_2$, Ach. Mot. Ta.Mot.	Tea. Perc. = 334.638 – 0.2183 Sel Per. – 1.0001 $L.S_1$ – 2.5205 $L.S_2$ – 3.1917 Ach. Mot. – 11.2342 Ta. Mot	0.9027	5.28	0.03
4.	Tea. Perc. Sel. Perc. $L.S_1$, $L.S_2$, $L.S_4$, Ach. Mot. Ta.Mot.	Tea. Perc. = 338.602 + 0.2350 Sel. Perc. – 1.0259 $L.S_1$ – 2.5517 $L.S_2$ – 0.0961 $L.S_4$ – 3.2025 Ach. Mot. – 11.3778 Ta.Mot.	0.9044	3.74	0.08
5.	Tea. Perc. Sel. Perc. $L.S_1$, $L.S_2$, $L.S_3$, $L.S_4$, Ach. Mot. Ta. Mot.	Tea. Perc. = 359.693 + 0.2099 Sel. Perc. – 1.1663 $L.S_1$ – 2.7221 $L.S_2$ – 0.1102 $L.S_3$ – 0.1690 $L.S_4$ – 3.2937 Ach. Mot. – 11.7277 Ta.Mot.	0.9047	2.58	0.18

Table 19: Single Regression Equations: Group: Talented Orthopedically Impaired Children
Dependent Variable—"Perception of Self"

Sl. No.	Name of the variables	The equations	R-Value	F-Value	Profb>F
1.	Sel. Perc., Ach. Mot.	Sel. Perc. = 112.050 + 0.9875 Ach. Mot.	0.2929	0.939	0.36
2.	Sel Perc., Ta. Mot.	Sel. Perc. = 116.25 + 1.00 Ta. Mot.	0.2045	0.436	0.52
3.	Sel. Perc., $L.S_1$	Sel. Perc. = 92.802 + 0.8012 $L.S_1$	0.7067	9.98	0.01
4.	Sel. Prec., $L.S_2$	Sel. Perc. = 143.411 – 0.8010 $L.S_2$	0.6277	6.503	0.02
5.	Sel. Perc., $L.S_3$	Sel. Perc. = 131.888 – 0.3759 $L.S_3$	0.4459	2.483	0.14
6.	Sel. Perc., $L.S_4$	Sel. Perc. = 120.009 + 0.0768 $L.S_4$	0.0849	0.073	0.70

Table 20: Double Regression Equations: Group: Talented orthopedically Impaired Children Dependent Variable—"Perception of Self"

S. No.	Name of the variables	The equations	R-Value	F-Value	Prob>F
1.	Sel. Perc., $L.S._1$, Ach. Mot.	Sel. Perc. = 82.584 + 0.7985 $L.S_1$ + 0.9675 Ach. Mot.	0.7628	6.263	0.01
2.	Sel. Perc., $L.S_1$, Ta. Mot.	Sel. Perc. = 84.890 + 0.8145 $L.S_1$ + 1.1714 Ta. Mot.	0.7462	5.652	0.02
3.	Sel. Perc., $L.S_2$, Ach. Mot.	Sel. Perc. = 133.846 – 0.7784 $L.S_2$ + 0.8415 Ach. Mot.	0.6754	3.773	0.06
4.	Sel. Perc., $L.S_2$, Ta. Mot.	Sel. Perc. = 149.008 – 0.8735 $L.S_2$ – 0.5862 Ta. Mot.	0.6329	3.065	0.09
5.	Sel. Perc., $L.S_3$, Ach. Mot.	Sel. Perc. = 122.564 – 0.351 $L.S_3$ + 0.8163 Ach. Mot.	0.5066	1.554	0.26
6.	Sel. Perc., $L.S_3$, Ta. Mot.	Sel. Perc. = 124.916 – 0.3894 $L.S_3$ + 1.1537 Ta. Mot.	0.5043	1.535	0.26
7.	Sel. Perc., $L.S_4$, Ach. Mot.	Sel. Perc. = 110.553 + 0.0507 $L.S_4$ + 0.9684 Ach. Mot.	0.2983	0.439	0.65
8.	Sel. Perc., $L.S_4$, Ta. Mot.	Sel. Perc. = 112.509 + 0.0997 $L.S_4$ + 1.0629 Ta. Mot.	0.2319	0.256	0.71

Table 21: Multiple Regression Equations Group: Talented Orthopedically Impaired Children Dependent Variable: "Perception of Self"

Sl. No.	Name of the variables	The equations	R-Value	F-Value	Prob>F
1.	Sel. Perc. L.S_1, Ach. Mot., Ta. Mot.	Sel. Perc. = 68.5375 +0.8162 L.S_1 +1.2529 Ach. Mot. +1.6334 Ta. Mot	0.8282	5.83	0.02
2.	Sel. Perc., L.S_1, L.S_3 Ach. Mot., Ta. Mot.	Sel. Perc. = 73.587 +0.7558 L.S_1 –0.0967 L.S_3 +1.2088 Ach. Mot. +1.6427 Ta. Mot.	0.8343	4.01	0.05
3.	Sel. Perc., L.S_1, L.S_2, L.S_3, Ach. Mot., Ta. Mot.	Sel. Perc. = 90.175 +0.6051 L.S_1 –0.2088 L.S_2 –0.148 L.S_3 +1.0708 Ach. Mot. +1.2014 Ta. Mot.	0.8379	2.83	0.11
4.	Sel. Perc., L.S_1, L.S_2, L.S_3, L.S_4, Ach. Mot.	Sel. Perc. = 144.807 +0.1742 L.S_1 +0.6880 L.S_2 –425 L.S_3 –0.2428 L.S_4 +0.7375 Ach. Mot.	0.8448	2.99	0.10
5.	Sel. Perc., L.S_1, L.S_2, L.S_3 L.S_4, Ach. Mot., Ta. Mot.	Sel. Perc. = 131.784 +0.2769 L.S_1 –0.5664 L.S_2 –0.369 L.S_3, –0.2014, L.S_4 +0.8319 Ach. Mot. +0.3543 Ta. Mot.	0.8454	2.09	0.21

impaired children could be made on the basis of their learning styles, namely, "active experimentation" and "concrete experience".

Table 20 shows the double regression equations and their analysis between "perception of self", each of the four "learning styles", "achievement motivation" and "task related motivation" of the talented orthopaedically impaired children. Each of the equations carries a pair of affective variables where perception of self has been considered as dependent variable. A deep study of the table reveals that among the all eight equations as shown here, only equation nos. 1-4 carry high R-values. The probability >F values possessed by equation numbers 1, 2, 3, and 4 are found 0.01, 0.02, 0.06 and 0.09 respectively. This indicates that the pairs of variables, namely, "active experimentation learning style" and "achievement motivation" "active experimentation". Learning style and "task related motivation", "concrete experience" learning style and "task related motivation"; "concrete experience" learning style and "achievement motivation" do affect the "perception of self" of the group. Since "active experimentation" learning style paired with either "achievement motivation" or "task related motivation" as shown in equation nos. 1 and 2, possess high predictive values, therefore, could be considered most suitable pair of affective variables for the purpose of prediction of the "perception of self" of the group. Here it could be explained that the prediction of "perception of self" of the group could be made on the basis of "active experimentation", the group's most preferred learning style as found earlier, paired with either "achievement motivation" or "task related motivation". This indicates that the prediction of "perception of self" of the talented orthopaedically impaired children could be made on the basis of their preferred learning style, and motivational characteristics "achievement motivation" and "task related motivation".

Table 21 shows the multiple regression equations between "perception of self", each of the four "learning styles", "achievement motivation", and "task related motivation" of the talented orthopaedically impaired children. A study of this table reveals that each of the equations as shown here possesses high R-values. However, prob>F values are only found significant in equation No. 1 and 2, carrying set of affective variables, namely, "active experimentation learning style", "achievement motivation" and "task related motivation", "active experimentation", "abstract conceptualisation" learning styles", "achievement motivation", and "task related motivation". This indicates that the above stated set of affective variables could be considered for the purpose of prediction of "perception of self" of the group. Therefore it could be said that prediction of "perception of self" of the talented orthopaedically impaired children could be made only on the basis of set of variables, namely, "active experimentation learning style", "achievement motivation", and "task related motivation", "active experimentation" "abstract conceptualisation", learning styles, "achievement motivation", and "task related motivation".

Simple, Double and Multiple Regression Equations and Their Analysis–Talented Visually Impaired Children

This sub-section deals with simple, double and multiple regression equations and their analysis among different variables of the talented visually impaired children. Calcualion of regression equations are done as follows:

(i) Simple, double, and multiple regression equations were calculated between "teacher's perception", "learning styles", "achievement motivation", and "task related motivation", where "teacher's perception" was considered as dependent variable and other variables as independent ones.

(ii) Simple, double, and multiple regression equations were calculated between "perception of self", "learning styles", "achievement motivation", and "task related motivation", where "perception of self" was considered as dependent variable and other variables as independent ones.

Regression equations are shown in Tables (22-27) followed by their analysis.

Tables 22-27 show the simple, double and multiple regression equations and their analysis of the talented visually impaired children between "teacher's perception" "perception of self", four "learning styles", "achievement motivation', and "task related motivation", where "teacher's perception" has been considered as dependent variable. A thorough study of table 22, depicting the simple regression equitations shows that among all

Table 22: Single Regression Equations: Group: Talented Visually Impaired Children Dependent Variable: "Teacher's Perception"

Sl. No.	Name of the variables	The equations	R-Value	F-Value	Prob>F
1.	Teac. Perc., Ach. Mot.	Teac. Perc. = 96.049 + 3.4427 Ach. Mot.	0.7874	16.315	0.002
2.	Teac. Perc., Ta. Mot.	Teac. Perc. = 164.922 – 3.4452 Ta. Mot.	0.6505	7.337	0.02
3.	Teac. Perc., $L.S_1$	Teac. Perc. = 163.277 – 0.7124 $L.S_1$	0.3362	1.239	0.29
4.	Teac. Perc., $L.S_2$	Teac. Perc. = 139.701 + 0.0786 $L.S_2$	0.0447	0.021	0.88
5.	Teac. Perc., $L.S_3$	Teac. Perc. = 126.54 + 0.5567 $L.S_3$	0.3679	1.566	0.23
6.	Teac. Perc., $L.S_4$	Teac. Perc. = 164.019 – 0.6027 $L.S_4$	0.2658	0.761	0.40
7.	Teac. Perc., Sel, Perc.	Teac. Perc. = 157.387 – 0.1353 Sel. Perc.	0.1145	0.133	0.72

Table 23. Double Regression Equations: Group: Talented Visually Impaired Children Dependent Variable—Teacher's Perception

Sl. No.	Name of the variables	The equations	R-Value	F-Value	Prob>F
1.	Teac. Perc., $L.S_1$, Ach. Mot.	Teac. Perc. = 109.754 – 0.3820 $L.S_1$ + 3.2831 Ach. Mot.	0.8065	8.370	0.008
2.	Teac. Perc., $L.S_1$ Ta. Mot.	Teac. Perc = 170.988 – 0.2484 $L.S_1$ –3.2276 Ta. Mot.	0.6595	3.463	0.07
3.	Teac. Perc., $L.S._2$ Ach. Mot	Teac. Perc. = 101.417 – 0.3521 $L.S_2$ + 3.702 Ach. Mot.	0.8109	8.631	0.008
4.	Teac. Perc., $L.S_2$ Ta. Mot.	Teac. Perc. = 164.285 + 0.0245 $L.S_2$ – 3.4416 Ta. Mot.	0.6507	3.304	0.08
5.	Teac. Perc., $L.S_3$ Ach. Mot.	Teac. Perc. = 83.867 + 0.4887 $L.S_3$ + 3.3601 Ach. Mot.	0.8509	11.803	0.03
6.	Teac. Perc., $L.S_3$ Ta. Mot.	Teac. Perc. = 159.985 + 0.2908 $L.S_3$ – 3.1437 Ta. Mot.	0.6759	3.786	0.06
7.	Teac. Perc., $L.S_4$ Ach. Mot.	Teac. Perc. = 106.943 – 0.2583 $L.S_4$ + 3.3437 Ach. Mot.	0.7953	7.744	0.01
8.	Teac. Perc., $L.S_4$ Ta. Mot.	Teac. Perc. = 187.88 – 0.6166 $L.S_4$ – 3.4587 Ta. Mot.	0.7051	4.449	0.04
9.	Teac. Perc., Sel. Perc., $L.S_1$,	Teac. Perc. = 158.75 + 0.0494 Sel. Perc. – 0.7525 $L.S_1$	0.3342	0.566	0.58
10.	Teac. Perc., Sel. Perc. $L.S_2$	Teac. Perc. = 162.499 – 0.1643 Sel. Perc. –0.0697 $L.S_2$	0.1192	0.065	0.93
11.	Teac. Perc., Sel. Perc. $L.S_3$	Teac. Perc. = 142.913 – 0.1415 Sel. Perc. + 0.5593 $L.S_3$	0.3870	0.793	0.48
12.	Teac. Perc., Sel. Perc., $L.S_4$	Teac. Perc. = 169.507 – 0.0563 Sel. Perc. – 0.5741 $L.S_4$	0.2698	0.353	0.71
13.	Teac. Perc., Ach. Mot. Sel. Perc.,	Teac. Perc. = 40.815 + 0.3959 Sel. Perc. + 4.1401 Ach. Mot.	0.8872	10.863	0.004
14.	Teac. Perc., Ta. Mot. Sel. Perc.,	Teac. Perc. = 182.171 – 0.1478 Sel. Perc. –3.4560 Ta. Mot.	0.6624	3.520	0.07

Table 24: Multiple Regression Equations: Group: Talented Visually Impaired Children Dependent Variable —"Teacher's Perception"

Sl. No.	Name of the variables	The equations	R-Value	F-Value	Prob>F
1.	Teac. Perc., Sel. Perc. $L.S_3$ Ach. Mot.	Teac. Perc. = 31.9114 + 0.3760 Sel. Perc. + 0.4683 $L.S_3$ + 4.0259 Ach. Mot.	0.8957	10.83	0.003
2.	Teac. Perc., Sel. Perc. $L.S_1$ Ach. Mot.	Teac. Perc. = 41.803 + 0.5870 Sel. Perc. –0.7707 $L.S_1$ +4.1545 Ach. Mot.	0.9002	11.40	0.002
3.	Teac. Perc., Sel. Perc. $L.S_1$ $L.S_4$, Ach. Mot.	Teac. Perc. = 61.174 + 0.7287 Sel. Perc. –1.007 $L.S_1$ –0.7267 $L.S_4$ + 4.0267 Ach. Mot	0.9464	15.00	0.001
4.	Teac. Perc., Sel. Perc. $L.S_1$ $L.S_4$, Ach. Mot. Ta. Mot.	Teac. Perc. = 40.3531 + 0.8488 Sel. Perc. –1.1799 $L.S_1$ –0.7583 $L.S_4$ + 4.5768 Ach. Mot. + 0.8742 Ta. Mot.	0.9516	11.52	0.004
5.	Teac. Perc., Sel. Perc. $L.S_1$ $L.S_3$, $L.S_4$, Ach. Mot. Ta. Mot	Teac. Perc. = 48.0044 + 1.0233 Sel. Perc. –1.6448 $L.S_1$ –0.3144 $L.S_3$ –1.00 $L.S_4$ + 4.7523 Ach. Mot. + 1.0871 Ta. Mot.	0.9582	9.36	0.01
6.	Teac. Perc., Sel. Perc. $L.S_1$ $L.S_2$, $L.S_3$, $L.S_4$, Ach. Mot	Teac. Perc. = 249.505 + 0.88 Sel. Perc. –2.9503 $L.S_1$ –1.4543 $L.S_2$ –1.7676 $L.S_3$ –2.4706 $L.S_4$ +4.1830 Ach. Mot.	0.9728	14.70	0.004
7.	Teac. Perc., Sel. Perc. $L.S_1$ $L.S_2$, $L.S_3$, $L.S_4$, Ach. Mot. Ta. Mot.	Teac. Perc. = 232.738 + 0.9187 Sel. Perc. –2.9159 $L.S_1$ – 1.3599 $L.S_2$ –1.6851 $L.S_3$ –2.3899 $L.S_4$ + 4.3315 Ach. Mot. + 0.2453 Ta. Mot.	0.9731	10.19	0.02

the seven equations only equation nos. 1 and 2 possess high R-values i.e., 0.7844 and 0.6505 respectively. The probability >F values for equation no. 1 is found to be 0.002 and for equqation no. 2 it is 0.02. This indicates that the variables taken in these two equations, namely, "achievement motivation", and "task related motivation" possess high affect on "teacher's perception" of the group. However, any of the four "learning styles", and "perception of self" of the group do not affect the group's "teacher's perception" so far as the R-values are concerned. Therefore, here it could be said that both "achievement motivation", and "task related motivation" of the group could be considered for the purpose of prediction of the "teacher's perception" of the talented visually impaired children as single variable(s).

Table 23 shows the double regression equations and their analysis between teacher's perception, "perception of self", each of the four "learning styles", "achievement motivation", and "task related motivation" of the talented visually impaired children. In all, 14 equations are shown in this table, each one carrying a pair of affective variables. A thorough study of this table reveals that the R-values possessed by equation nos. 1, 2, 3, 4, 5, 6, 7, 8, 13 and 14 are found high. However, the R-values possessed by equation no.s. 2, 4, 6, 14 are found to be significant below the desired level. The F-values possessed by equation nos. 1, 3, 5, 7, 8, 13 are found to be highly significant. This indicates that the pairs of variables taken in equation nos. 1, 3, 5, 7, 8 and 13 are highly affective on the group's "teacher's perception", Thus the pairs of variables on the basis of which "teacher's perception" of the talented visually impaired children could be made are ("active experimentation learning style", "achievement motivation"); (concrete experience learning style", "achievement motivation",); (abstract conceptualisation learning style", "achievement motivation") ("reflective observation learning style", "achievement motivation",); reflective observation learning style", "task related motivation"); and ("perception of self", "achievement motivation"). In short it could be said that teacher's perception of the talented visually impaired children could be made on the basis of their "perception of self" paired with "achievement motivation"; and the group's preferred learning styles paired with "achievement motivation" as well as "task related motivation".

Table 24 shows the multiple regression equations and their analysis between "teacher's perception", "perception of self", "learning styles", "achievement motivation", and "task related motivation" of the talented visually impaired children. In all seven equations are shown in this table each one carrying a set of affective variables and "teacher's perception" has been taken as dependent variable. A deep study of this table shows that all the equations shown in this table possess high R-values. The F-values possessed by these equations are found to be highly significant. Therefore the set of variables which could be considered for the purpose of prediction of teacher's perception of the talented visually impaired children are "perception of self", "abstract conceptualisation" learning style "achievement motivation", "perception of self", "active experimentation learning style", "achievement motivation"; "perception of self", "active experimentation learning style", "reflective observation learning style', "achievement motivation", "task related motivation"; ("perception of self" learning S1, learning S4, "achievement motivation', and "task related motivation", "perception of self", LS1, LS3, LS4 "achievement motivation" and "perception of self", LS1, LS2, LS3, L.S4 "achievement motivation", and "task related motivation'. This shows that prediction of teacher's perception of the talented visually impaired children could be made on the basis of the group's "perception of self"; preferred "learning style" and "motivational characteristics" conjointly.

Table 25 shows the simple regression equations between "perception of self", each of the four "learning styles', "achievement motivation', and "task related motivation" of the talented visually impaired children. Each equation carries two variables where "perception of self" has been considered as dependent variable. A deep study of this table shows that among all the six equations as shown here, only equation no. 4 possesses high R-value whose F-value is found significant. This indicates that only "concrete experience" learning style appears to affect the dependent variable, while other three "learning styles", "achievement motivation", and "task related motivation' do not possess the desired strength which could be used for the purpose of prediction of the group's "perception of self". Therefore it could be said that the single affective variable on the basis of which "perception of self" of the talented visually impaired children could be made is "concrete experience" learning style. Or in other words it could be said that prediction of "perception of self" of the talented visually impaired children could not be made on the basis of the group's most preferred learning style i.e. "reflective observation".

Table 25: Single Regression Equations: Group: Talented Visually Impaired Children Dependent Variable– "Perception of Self"

Sl. No.	Name of the variable	The equations	R-Value	F-Value	Prob>F
1.	Sel. Perc., Ach. Mot.	Sel. Perc. = 139.502 – 1.7611 Ach. Mot.	0.4754	2.92	0.11
2.	Sel. Perc., Ta. Mot.	Sel. Perc. = 116.659 – 0.0729 Ta. Mot.	0.0173	0.003	0.96
3.	Sel. Perc., $L.S_1$	Sel. Perc. = 91.551 + 0.8115 $L.S_1$	0.4463	2.488	0.14
4.	Sel. Perc., $L.S_2$	Sel. Perc. = 138.729 – 0.9025 $L.S_2$	0.6129	6.015	0.03
5.	Sel. Perc., $L.S_3$	Sel. Perc. = 115.67 + 0.0182 $L.S_3$	0.0141	0.002	0.96
6.	Sel. Perc., $L.S_4$	Sel. Perc. = 97.352 + 0.5073 $L.S_4$	0.2642	0.750	0.40

Table 26 depicts the double regression equations and their analysis between "perception of self", each of the four "learning styles", "achievement motivation", and "task related motivation" of the talented visually impaired children. In all, nine (9) equations are shown in this table each one carrying a pair of affective variables and "perception of self" as dependent variable. A thorough study of this table reveals that among all the equations only equation nos. 3 and 9 possess high R-values, whose F-values are found significant. It indicates that the pairs of variables taken in equation nos. 3 and 9, namely, "concrete experience" "learning style, "achievement motivation", and "active experimentation" and "concrete experience" learning style appear to affect the dependent variable i.e., "perception of self". The pairs of variables as shown in other equations since do not carry significant F-values and high R-values, therefore could not be considered for the purpose of prediction of perception of self. Here it could be said that, prediction of "perception of self" of the talented visually impaired children could be made on the basis of only two pairs of variables, namely, "concrete experience learning style", "achievement motivation", "active experimentation" and "concrete experience" learning style.

Table 27 shows multiple regression equations and their analysis between "perception of self", "learning styles", "achievement motivation", and "task related motivation" of the talented visually impaired children, carrying "perception of self" as dependent variable. Among the four (4) equations as shown in this table the equation nos. 1, 2, 3 possess high R-values and whose F-values are found highly significant. This indicates that the set of variables taken in the above said three equations affect the "perception of self". Therefore, the purpose of set of variables found suitable for the purpose of prediction of "perception of self" of the talented visually impaired children are "active experimentation" and "concrete experience learning styles", "achievement motivation" active experimentation" and "concrete experience", "learning styles and "achievement motivation" along with "task related motivation"; "active experimentation", "concrete experience", "abstract conceptualisation", learning styles, "achievement motivation" and "task related motivation". This shows that "learning styles" and "motivational characteristics" of the talented visually impaired children could be considered

Table 26: Double Regression Equations: Group: Talented Visually Impaired Children Dependent Variable—"Perception of Self"

Sl. No.	Name of the variables	The equations	R-Value	F-Value	Prob>F
1.	Sel. Perc., L.S_1 Ach. Mot.	Sel. Perc. = 115.752 + 0.6621 L.S_1 – 1.4844 Ach. Mot.	0.5924	2.456	0.14
2.	Sel. Perc., L.S_1, Ta. Mot.	Sel. Perc. = 93.693 + 0.9404 L.S_1 – 0.8967 Ta. Mot.	0.4839	1.376	0.30
3.	Sel. Perc., L.S_2, Ach. Mot.	Sel. Perc. = 151.132 – 0.7629 L.S_2 + 1.1994 Ach. Mot.	0.6866	4.013	0.05
4.	Sel. Perc., L.S_2, Ta. Mot.	Sel. Perc. = 140.195 – 0.9057 L.S_2 – 0.2052 Ta. Mot.	0.6146	2.731	0.11
5.	Sel. Perc., L.S_3, Ach. Mot.	Sel. Perc. = 138.153 + 0.0541 L.S_3 – 1.7703 Ach. Mot.	0.4773	1.327	0.31
6.	Sel. Perc., L.S_3 Ta. Mot.	Sel. Perc. = 116.206 + 0.0132 L.S_3 – 0.0592 Ta. Mot.	0.02	0.002	.99
7.	Sel. Perc., L.S_4 Ach. Mot.	Sel. Perc. = 125.195 + 0.3393 L.S_4 – 1.6311 Ach. Mot.	0.5059	1.548	0.26
8.	Sel. Perc., L.S_4 Ta.Mot	Sel. Perc. = 97.779 + 0.5071 L.S_4 – 0.0618 Ta. Mot.	0.2646	0.338	0.72
9.	Sel. Perc., L.S_1, L.S_2	Sel. Perc. = 114.45 + 0.7901 L.S_1 – 0.8900 L.S_2	0.7513	5.83	0.02

Table 27: Multiple Regression Equations: Group: Talented Visually Impaired Children Dependent Variable—"Perception of Self"

Sl. No.	Name of the variables	The equations	R-Value	F-Value	Prob>F
1.	Sel. Perc., $L.S_1$, $L.S_2$ Ach. Mot.	Sel. Perc. = 126.288 + 0.7033 $L.S_1$ − 0.7882 $L.S_2$ − 0.8868 Ach. Mot.	0.7839	4.25	0.04
2.	Sel. Perc., $L.S_1$, $L.S_2$ Ach. Mot., Ta. Mot.	Sel. Perc. = 148.35 + 0.9407 $L.S_1$ − 0.6888 $L.S_2$ − 2.0388 Ach. Mot. −2.4411 Ta. Mot.	0.8817	6.51	0.01
3.	Sel. Perc., $L.S_1$, $L.S_2$, $L.S_3$, Ach. Mot., Ta.Mot.	Sel. Perc. = 153.623 + 0.8763 $L.S_1$ − 0.7341 $L.S_2$ − 0.0717 $L.S_3$ − 2.0317 Ach. Mot. −2.4669 Ta.Mot.	0.8885	4.50	0.04
4.	Sel. Perc., $L.S_1$, $L.S_2$, $L.S_3$, $L.S_4$, Ach. Mot.	Sel. Perc. = 155.5708 + 0.8608 $L.S_1$ −0.7481 $L.S_2$ −0.0931$L.S_3$ −0.0166 $L.S_4$ −2.0351 Ach. Mot.	0.8885	3.13	0.11

conjointly for the purpose of prediction of "perception of self" of the group.

Simple, Double and Multiple Regression Equations and Their Analysis—Talented Speech and Hearing Impaired Children

This sub-section deals with simple, double and multiple regression equations and their analysis among different variables of the talented speech and hearing impaired children. Calculation of regression equations are done as follows:

(i) Simple, double, and multiple regression equations were calculated between "teacher's perception", "learning styles", "achievement motivation", and "task related motivation", where "teacher's perception" was considered as dependent variable and other variables as independent ones.

(ii) Simple, double and multiple regression equations were calculated between ".perception of self", "learning styles", "achievement motivation" and "task related motivation", where "perception of self" was considered as dependent variable and other variables as independent ones.

Regression equations are shown in the below given tables 28 to 33 followed by their analysis.

Tables 28 to 33 shows the simple, double and multiple regression equations between "teacher's perception", "perception of self" each of the four "learning styles", "achievement motivation", and "task related motivation", where "teacher's perception" has been considered as dependent variable. A look at table 28 reveals that among all seven (7) simple regression equations only equation no. 3 varying "active experimentation" learning style as affective variable possesses high R-value and whose F-value is found to be significant. It indicates that "active experimentation" learning style appears as the only single variable that affects "teacher's perception" of the group. It reflects that "active experimentation" as found earlier the group's most preferred learning style could be considered as the only single affective variable for the purpose of prediction of "teacher's perception" of the talented speech and hearing impaired children.

Table 28: Single Regression Equations: Group: Talented Speech and Hearing Impaired Children, Dependent Variable: "Teacher's Perception"

Sl. No.	Name of the variables	The equations	R-Value	F-Value	Prob>F
1.	Teac. Perc., Ach. Mot.	Teac. Perc. = 155.42 – 0.7102 Ach. Mot.	0.0632	0.040	0.84
2.	Teac. Perc., Ta. Mot.	Teac. Perc. = 166.491 – 2.5964 Ta. Mot.	0.2931	0.939	0.35
3.	Teac. Perc., $L.S_1$	Teac. Perc. = 191.658 – 1.1889 $L.S_1$	0.5656	4.727	0.05
4.	Teac. Perc., $L.S_2$	Teac. Perc. = 111.321 + 1.4252$L.S_2$	0.3911	1.876	0.20
5.	Teac. Perc., $L.S_3$	Teac. Perc. = 137.511 + 0.4953$L.S_3$	0.2661	0.763	0.40
6.	Teac. Perc., $L.S_4$	Teac. Perc. = 140.706 + 0.1885$L.S_4$	0.0606	0.037	0.85
7.	Teac. Perc., Sel. Perc.	Teac. Perc. = 179.133 – 0.2766 Sel. Perc.	0.2655	0.758	0.40

Table 29 depicts the double regression equations and their analysis among "teacher's perception", "perception of self", each of the four "learning styles", "achievement motivation", and "task related motivation" of the talented speech and hearing impaired children. In all fifteen (15) equations, each one carrying a pair of affective variables and "teacher's perception" as dependent variable are shown in this table. A thorough study of this table reveals that except equation no. 15, all other equations possess low R-values along with non-significant F-values. This indicates that the pair of variables taken in equation no. 15 namely, "active experimentation ($L.S_1$)", and "concrete experience" ($L.S_2$), learning styles one found affective ones so far as "teacher's perception" of the group is concerned. Therefore it could be noted that the prediction of "teacher's perception" of the talented speech and hearing impaired children could be made only on the basis of a single pair of affective variables, namely, "active experimentation" and "concrete experience" learning styles. However, "achievement motivation" and "task related motivation" do not affect teacher's perception of the talented speech and hearing impaired children.

Table 30 shows the multiple regression equations and their analysis between "teacher's perception, "perception of self", each of the four "learning styles", "achievement motivation", and "task related motivation" of the talented speech and hearing impaired children. In all there are six (6) equations shown in this table each one carrying a set of affective variables and "teacher's perception" as dependent variable. A deep study of this table reveals that each of these equations possess high R-values and non-significant F-values. This indicates that the set of affective variables taken in these equations could not be used as predictive ones, despite the fact that each one of them possesses high R-values. Therefore, it could be said that "perception of self", "learning styles", "achievement motivation", and "task related motivation" of the talented speech and hearing impaired children do not conjointly affect their "teacher's perception", hence could not be considered for the purpose of prediction.

Table 31 shows the simple regression equations and their analysis between "perception of self", each of the four "learning styles", "achievement motivation", and "task related motivation" of the talented speech and hearing impaired children. In all, six

Table 29: Double Regression Equations: Group: Talented Speech and Hearing Impaired Children Dependent Variable: "Teacher's Perception"

Sl. No.	Name of the variables	The equations	R-Value	F-Value	Prob>F
1.	Teac. Perc., $L.S_1$, Ach. Mot.	Teac. Perc. = 218.114 – 1.2731 $L.S_1$ –2.1381 Ach. Mot.	0.5965	2.486	0.13
2.	Teac. Perc., $L.S_1$, Ta. Mot.	Teac. Perc. = 198.922 – 1.1042 $L.S_1$ – 1.4340 Ta. Mot.	0.5879	2.376	0.14
3.	Teac. Perc., $L.S_2$, Ach. Mot.	Teac. Perc. = 87.809 + 1.6569 $L.S_2$ + 1.6125 Ach. Mot.	0.4177	0.952	0.42
4.	Teac. Perc., $L.S_2$, Ta. Mot.	Teac. Perc. = 128.403 + 1.8429 $L.S_2$ –3.8251 Ta. Mot.	0.5751	2.224	0.16
5.	Teac. Perc., $L.S_3$, Ach. Mot.	Teac. Perc. = 155.973 + 0.5973 $L.S_3$ –1.8826 Ach. Mot.	0.31	0.478	0.63
6.	Teac. Perc., $L.S_3$, Ta. Mot.	Teac. Perc. = 153.664 + 0.4273 $L.S_3$ – 2.3115 Ta. Mot.	0.3709	0.718	0.51
7.	Teac. Perc., $L.S_4$, Ach. Mot.	Teac. Perc. = 148.492 + 0.2242 $L.S_4$ –0.8339 Ach. Mot.	0.0954	0.041	0.95
8.	Teac. Perc., $L.S_4$, Ta. Mot.	Teac. Perc. = 173.905 – 0.1669 $L.S_4$ – 2.7692 Ta.Mot.	0.2973	0.436	0.65
9.	Teac. Perc., Sel. Perc., $L.S_1$,	Teac. Perc. = 195.201 – 0.0425 Sel. Perc. – 1.1539 $L.S_1$	0.5678	2.141	0.17
10.	Teac. Perc., Sel. Perc. $L.S_2$	Teac. Perc. = 148.442 – 0.4025 Sel. Perc. + 1.7653 $L.S_2$	0.5462	1.913	0.20
11.	Teac. Perc., Sel. Perc. $L.S_3$	Teac. Perc. = 167.128 – 0.2526 Sel. Perc. + 0.4527$L.S_3$	0.393	0.667	0.53
12.	Teac. Perc., Sel. Pec., $L.S_4$	Teac. Perc. = 225.161 – 0.4445 Sel. Perc. – 0.7293 $L.S_4$	0.3148	0.495	0.62
13.	Teac. Perc., Ach. Mot. Sel. Perc.,	Teac. Perc. = 195.026 – 0.2953 Sel. Perc. – 1.2503 Ach. Mot.	0.2874	0.045	0.67
14.	Teac. Perc., Ta. Mot. Sel. Perc.,	Teac. Perc. = 181.018 – 0.1711 Sel. Perc. – 1.9148 Ta. Mot.	0.3269	0.539	0.60
15.	Teac. Perc., $L.S_1$, $L.S_2$	Teac. Perc. = 155.45 – 1.1834 $L.S_1$+ 1.4116$L.S_2$	0.6890	4.09	0.05

Table 30: Multiple Regression Equations: Group: Talented Speech and Hearing Impaired Children; Dependent Variable: "Teacher's Perception"

Sl. No.	Name of the variables	The equations	R-Value	F-Value	Prob>F
1.	Teac. Perc., $L.S_2$, $L.S_3$ Ta. Mot.	Teac. Perc. = 85.711 + 2.6822 $L.S_2$ + 1.0005 $L.S_3$ –3.7176 Ta. Mot.	0.7505	3.44	0.07
2.	Teac. Perc., Sel. Perc. $L.S_2$, $L.S_3$, Ta. Mot.	Teac. Perc. = 105.95 – 0.2749 Sel. Perc. + 2.8156 $L.S_2$ +1.0145 $L.S_3$ – 2.7020 Ta. Mot.	0.7852	2.81	0.11
3.	Teac. Perc , Sel. Perc. $L.S_2$ $L.S_3$ Ach. Mot., Ta. Mot.	Teac. Perc. = 96.465 – 0.2678 Sel. Perc. +2.2678 $L.S_2$ + 0.9961 $L.S_3$ + 0.6763 Ach. Mot. – 2.7618 Ta. Mot.	0.7870	1.95	0.21
4.	Teac. Perc., Sel. Perc. $L.S_1$, $L.S_2$, $L.S_3$, Ach. Mot., Ta Mot.	Teac. Perc. = 84.923 – 0.3084 Sel. Perc. + 0.1997 $L.S_1$ + 3.0892 $L.S_2$ + 1.1515 $L.S_3$ + 0.7844 Ach. Mot. – 2.8289 Ta. Mot.	0.7879	1.36	0.37
5.	Teac. Perc., Sel. Perc. $L.S_1$ $L.S_2$, $L.S_3$, $L.S_4$, Ta. Mot	Teac. Perc. = –278.402 – 0.2358 Sel. Perc. + 3.1685 $L.S_1$ + 5.9470 $L.S_2$ + 4.3151 $L.S_3$ + 3.1434 $L.S_4$ – 2.8268 Ta. Mot.	0.7971	1.45	0.34
6.	Teac. Perc., Sel. Perc. $L.S_1$, $L.S_2$, $L.S_3$, $L.S_4$, Ach. Mot., Ta. Mot.	Teac. Perc. = –267.2235 – 0.2424 Sel. Perc. + 3.0511 $L.S_1$ + 5.8806 $L.S_2$ + 4.1697 $L.S_3$ + 2.9828 $L.S_3$ + 0.4437 Ach. Mot. – 2.8725 Ta. Mot.	0.7978	1.00	0.53

Table 31: Single Regression Equations: Group: Talented Speech and Hearing Impaired Children; Dependent Variable: "Perception of Self"

Sl. No.	Name of the variables	The equations	R-Value	F-Value	Prob>F
1.	Sel. Perc., Ach. Mot.	Sel. Perc. = 133.644 – 1.8224 Ach. Mot.	0.1634	0.296	0.59
2.	Sel. Perc., Ta. Mot.	Sel. Perc. = 84.877 + 3.9824 Ta. Mot.	0.4684	2.810	0.12
3.	Sel. Perc., $L.S_1$	Sel. Perc. = 83.305 + 0.8228 $L.S_1$	0.4085	2.004	0.18
4.	Sel. Perc., $L.S_2$	Sel. Perc. = 92.206 + 0.8448 $L.S_2$	0.2455	0.641	0.44
5.	Sel. Perc., $L.S_3$	Sel. Perc. = 117.208 – 0.1687 $L.S_3$	0.0943	0.090	0.77
6.	Sel. Perc., $L.S_4$	Sel. Perc. = 189.965 – 2.0645 $L.S_4$	0.6892	9.063	0.01

(6) equations are shown and among them only equation no. 6 carrying "reflective observation' learning style possesses high R-value and its F-value is found highly significant. This indicates that "reflective observation", the group's second preferred learning style as found earlier, is found as the only single variable that affects the group's "perception of self". Thus, it could be said that "perception of self" of the talented speech and hearing impaired children could be predicted on the basis of their second preferred learning style i.e. "reflective observation".

Table 32 depicts the double regression equations and their analysis between "perception of self", each of the four "learning styles", "achievement motivation", and "task related motivation", where "perception of self" has been considered as the dependent variable. Among the nine (9) equations as shown in this table only equation nos. 7, 8, 9 possess high R-values which are found significant. This indicates that the pairs of variables, taken in these three equations, namely, "$L.S_4$", "achievement motivation"; "$L.S_4$", "task related motivation"; and "$L.S_3$", "$L.S_4$" are found affective ones so far as "perception of self" of the group is concerned. Therefore, it could be said that "perception of self" of the talented speech and hearing impaired children could be predicted on the basis of the pairs of variables, namely, "reflective observation,, "learning style", "achievement motivation"; "reflective observation" learning style, "task related motivation"; "reflective observation" and "abstract conceptualisation" learning styles. This shows that prediction of "perception of self" of the talented speech and hearing impaired children could be made on the basis of their preferred "learning styles" and "motivational characteristics".

Table 33 shows the multiple regression equations and their analysis between "perception of self", each of the four "learning styles", "achievement motivation", and "task related motivation" of the talented speech and hearing impaired children. In all five (5) equations are shown in this table each one carrying a set of affective variables and "perception of self" as the dependent variable. A thorough study of this table depicts that each of these five equations possesses high R-values. An analysis of the F-values reveals that among all these equations only equation no. 1 is found to be significant. This indicates that the set of variables taken in equation no. 1, namely, "abstract conceptualisation" ($L.S_3$)

Table 32: Double Regression Equations: Group: Talented Speech and Hearing Impaired Children; Dependent Variable: "Perception of Self"

Sl. No.	Name of the variables	The equations	R-Value	F-Value	Prob>V
1.	Sel. Perc., $L.S_1$, Ach. Mot.	Sel. Perc. = 94.950 + 0.7857 $L.S_1$ – 0.9411 Ach. Mot.	0.4175	0.950	0.42
2.	Sel. Perc., $L.S_1$, Ta. Mot.	Sel. Perc. = 66.474 + 0.6266 $L.S_1$ + 3.3228 Ta. Mot.	0.5569	2.023	0.18
3.	Sel. Perc., $L.S_2$, Ach. Mot	Sel. Perc. = 103.857 + 0.73 $L.S_2$ – 0.7990 Ach. Mot.	0.2544	0.311	0.74
4.	Sel. Perc., $L.S_2$, Ta. Mot.	Sel. Perc. = 75.739 + 0.4421 $L.S_2$ + 3.6876 Ta. Mot.	0.4844	1.380	0.30
5.	Sel. Perc., $L.S_3$, Ach. Mot.	Sel. Perc. = 133.572 – 0.0783 $L.S_3$ – 1.6687 Ach. Mot.	0.1746	0.141	0.87
6.	Sel. Perc., $L.S_3$, Ta. Mot.	Sel. Perc. = 86.210 – 0.0526 $L.S_3$ + 3.9473 Ta. Mot.	0.4692	1.271	0.32
7.	Sel. Perc., $L.S_4$, Ach. Mot.	Sel. Perc. = 196.507 – 2.0345 $L.S_4$ – 0.7005 Ach. Mot.	0.6925	4.147	0.05
8.	Sel. Perc., $L.S_4$, Ta. Mot.	Sel. Perc. = 164.451 – 1.7913 $L.S_4$ + 2.1282 Ta. Mot.	0.7278	5.069	0.03
9.	Sel. Perc., $L.S_3$, $L.S_4$	Sel. Perc. = 214.000 – 0.6069 $L.S_3$ – 2.3787 $L.S_4$	0.7615	6.21	0.02

Table 33: Multiple Regression Equations: Group: Talented Speech and Hearing Impaired Children; Dependent; Variable: "Perception of Self"

Sl. No.	Name of the variables	The equations	R-Value	F-Value	Prob>F
1.	Sel. Perc., L.S_3, L.S_4 Ta. Mot	Sel. Perc. = 193.966 – 0.5247 L.S_3 –2.1565 L.S_4 + 1.4004 Ta. Mot.	0.7756	4.03	0.05
2.	Sel. Perc., L.S_3, L.S_4, Ach. Mot., Ta. Mot.	Sel. Perc. = 190.6133 – 0.5717 L.S_3 – 2.2155 L.S_4 + 0.6342 Ach. Mot. + 1.3413 Ta. Mot.	0.7774	2.67	0.12
3.	Sel. Perc., L.S_1, L.S_3, L.S_4 Ach. Mot., Ta. Mot.	Sel. Perc. = 207.766 – 0.2155 L.S_1 – 0.7583 L.S_3 + 0.8585 Ach. Mot. + 1.2545 Ta. Mot.	0.7789	1.85	0.23
4.	Sel. Perc., L.S_1, L.S_2, L.S_3, L.S_4, Ta. Mot.,	Sel. Perc. = 440.6345 – 2.0909 L.S_1 – 2.0190 L.S_2 – 2.6760 L.S_3 – 4.1608 L.S_4, + 1.4386 Ta. Mot.	0.7815	1.88	0.23
5.	Sel. Perc., L.S_1, L.S_2, L.S_3 L.S_4 Ach. Mot. Ta. Mot.,	Sel. Perc. = 458.2151 – 2.311 L.S_1 – 2.1317 L.S_2 – 2.9476 L.S_3 – 4.4437 L.S_4, + 0.9436 Ach. Mot. + 1.3213 Ta. Mot.	0.7849	1.34	0.32

learning style, "reflective observation" ($L.S_4$) learning style, and "task related motivation" conjointly affect the "perception of self" of the group. Therefore it could be said that these three self of variables conjointly could be considered for the purpose of prediction of "perception of self" of the talented speech and hearing impaired children.

Summary of Findings

The researcher after analysis and interpretation of the data has reached at the following major findings. These findings have relevance with respect to objectives of the study. This sub-section consists of the following parts:

Teacher's perception of the talented exceptional children

Teacher's perception of the talented orthopaedically impaired, visually impaired and speech and hearing impaired children is found high.

Status of the talented exceptional children on "perception of self" "learning styles", and "motivational characteristcs".

I. Talented Orthopaedically Impaired Children

1. The talented orthopaedically impaired children possess low but positive "perception of self".
2. Compared to "social self", these children possess high "academic self" but low "physical self".
3. The predominant learning style of the talented orthopaedically impaired children is "active experimentation". They emphasise on practical applications as opposed to reflective understanding. They are willing to take some risk to achieve their learning objectives and want to see the learning outcomes.
4. The talented orthopaedically impaired children possess low achievement motivation associated with anxiety.

The above findings uphold the hypothesis that "the talented orthopaedically impaired children possess low perception of self and low achievement motivation".

II. Talented Visually Impaired Children

1. The talented visually impaired children possess low but positive "perception of self".

2. Compared to "social self", the group possesses high "academic self" but low "physical self".
3. The predominant learning style of the talented visually impaired children is "reflective observation". During learning phase these children emphasise on understanding as opposed to practical application. They like to rely on their own thoughts and feelings to form opinions.
4. The talented visually impaired children possess moderate achievement motivation.

Finding no. 1 upholds the hypothesis that the "talented visually impaired children possess low perception of self". Finding no. 4 rejects the hypothesis that the talented visually impaired children possess low achievement motivation.

III. Talented Speech and Hearing Impaired Children

1. The talented speech and hearing impaired children possess low but positive "perception of self".
2. Compared to "social self", these children possess high "academic self" but low "physical self".
3. The predominant learning styles of the talented speech and hearing impaired children are "active experimentation" and "reflective observation". These children emphasise both on practical applications as well as on reflective understanding during learning depending on the nature of different learning tasks.
4. The talented speech and hearing impaired children possess low "achievement motivation" associated with "anxiety".

Findings no. 1 and 4 support to uphold the hypothesis that, "the talented speech and hearing impaired children possess low "perception of self" and "low achievement motivation".

I. Statistical Comparisons

Comparison between talented orthopaedically impaired and talented visually impaired children.

1. The talented orthopaedically impaired and talented visually impaired children differ significantly on "teacher's

perception". The previous group is found superior to the latter one with regard to "teacher's perception".

2. There is a significant difference between the two groups on "perception of self" and the talented orthopaedically impaired children possess higher "perception of self" than the talented visually impaired children.
3. On "academic self" both the groups differ significantly. And the talented orthopaedically impaired children possess higher academic self than the talented visually impaired children.
4. No significant differences are found between the two groups on "social self" and "physical self". Neither of the group is found superior to the other in perceiving their social traits and physical abilities.
5. Among the four learning styles, the talented orthopaedically impaired children differ significantly from the talented visually impaired children only on one learning style i.e. "active experimentation". On other three learning styles no group variations are found.
6. The talented visually impaired children differ significantly from the talented orthopaedically impaired children on "achievement motivation". The previous group possesses higher "achievement motivation" than the latter one.

The above-said findings reflect that the hypothesis that "the talented orthopaedically impaired and talented visually impaired children do not differ significantly on (i) "perception of self", preferred "learning styles", and on "achievement motivation" is thus rejected.

II. Comparison between talented orthopaedically Impaired and Talented Speech and Hearing Impaired Children

1. There is no significant difference between the talented orthopaedically impaired and talented speech and hearing impaired children on "teacher's perception". This finding supports to uphold the hypothesis that "the talented orthopaedically impaired and talented speech and hearing

impaired children do not differ significantly on teacher's perception".

2. The two groups differ significantly on "perception of self". The talented orthopaedically impaired children possess higher "perception of self" than the talented speech and hearing impaired children. This finding rejects the hypothesis that the talented orthopaedically and talented speech and hearing impaired children do not differ significantly on "perception of self".

3. On "academic self" and "social self" the two groups differ significantly. This indicates that the talented orthopaedically impaired children compared to the talented speech and hearing impaired children possess better perception of their academic abilities and social traits.

4. The talented orthopaedically impaired and talented speech and hearing impaired children do not differ significantly on "physical self". This indicates that both the groups perceive their physical abilities and strengths at the same level.

5. The two groups differ significantly on their least preferred learning style i.e. "abstract conceptualisation". The talented orthopaedically impaired children appear to be superior in abstract thinking ability to the talented speech and hearing impaired children.

6. The two groups do not differ significantly on their most preferred learning styles i.e., "active experimentation and reflective observation". This finding supports to uphold the hypothesis that "the talented orthopaedically impaired and talented speech and hearing impaired children do not differ significantly on their preferred learning styles."

7. On "achievement motivation", and on "task related motivation" the talented orthopaedically impaired children do not differ significantly from the talented speech and hearing impaired children. This indicates that neither of the group is superior to the other in relation to their "achievement motivation" and "task related motivation". This also supports to uphold the hypothesis that "the talented orthopaedically impaired children do not differ significantly

from the talented speech and hearing impaired children on their "achievement motivation".

III. Comparison between Talented Visually Impaired and Talented Speech and Hearing Impaired Children

1. On teacher's perception the two groups do not differ significantly. Thus the hypothesis that "the talented visually impaired children and the talented speech and hearing impaired children do not differ significantly on "teacher's perception" is upheld.
2. On "perception of self" no significant difference between the two groups is found. This indicates that both the talented speech and hearing impaired and talented visually impaired children perceive their abilities, strengths, desires and goals of life at the same rate. The hypothesis that "the talented visually impaired children do not differ significantly from the talented speech and hearing impaired children on perception of self', thus is upheld.
3. The talented visually impaired and speech and hearing impaired children do not differ significantly on three facts of self, namely, "academic self", "social self" and "physical self". This shows that neither of the group is superior to the other in perceiving their academic abilities, social traits and physical abilities.
4. The two groups differ significantly on two learning styles, namely, "active experimentation" and "abstract conceptualisation". This finding supports to reject the hypothesis that "the talented speech and hearing impaired children do not differ significantly form the talented visually impaired children on their preferred learning styles".
5. The two groups differ significantly on "achievement motivation". This indicates that the talented visually impaired children are more achievement oriented than the talented speech and hearing impaired children. Thus, the hypothesis that "the talented visually impaired children do not differ significantly from the talented speech and hearing impaired children on achievement motivation" is rejected.

Correlational Studies

I. Group—Talented Orthopaedically Impaired Children

1. Teacher's perception of the talented orthopaedically impaired children correlates positively with the group's "perception of self" and "preferred learning style". This indicates that there exists a positive relationship between "teacher's perception", perception of self and preferred "learning styles" of the talented orthopaedically impaired children. Thus the hypothesis is upheld, that "there is a positive correlation between "teacher's perception and perception of self of the talented orthopaedically impaired children."
2. Teacher's perception of the group correlates negatively with the group's "achievement motivation". This rejects the hypothesis that "there is a positive correlation among "teacher's perception" and "achievement motivation" of the talented orthopaedically impaired children.
3. There is a significant positive correlation found among the perception of self and the preferred "learning styles" of the group. This supports to uphold the hypothesis that "there is a positive correlation among perception of self and preferred learning style of the talented orthopaedically impaired children."
4. The "perception of self" of the group correlates positively with the group's "achievement motivation". Thus the hypothesis is upheld that "there is a positive correlation among perception of self and achievement motivation of the talented orthopaedically impaired children."

II. Talented Visually Impaired Children

1. The "teacher's perception" of the talented visually impaired children correlates negatively with the group's "perception of self" and preferred learning style. This shows that there is no relationship between teacher's perception of the talented visually impaired children with their "perception of self" and preferred "learning styles". Thus the hypothesis

is rejected that "teacher's perception" has positive correlation with perception of self and preferred learning style of the talented visually impaired children."

2. Teacher's perception of the group correlates with the group's "achievement motivation". This finding supports to uphold the hypothesis that "there is a positive correlation between teacher's perception and achievement motivation of the talented visually impaired children".

3. "Perception of self" of the group correlates positively with the group's preferred "learning style". This finding supports to uphold the hypothesis that there is positive correlation among perception of self and preferred learning style of the talented usually impaired children.

4. "Perception of self" of the group correlates negatively with the group's "achievement motivation". This indicates that there is no relationship among perception of self and achievement motivation of the group. Thus, the hypothesis that "there is positive correlation between perception of self and achievement motivation of the talented visually impaired children" is rejected.

III. Talented Speech and Hearing Impaired Children

1. "Teacher's perception" of the talented speech and hearing impaired children negatively correlates with the group's "perception of self", "preferred learning style" and "achievement motivation". This finding supports to reject the hypothesis that "there is a positive correlation among teacher's perception, perception of self, preferred learning style and achievement motivation of the talented speech and hearing impaired children".

2. "Perception of self" of the group shows negative correlation with the group's most preferred learning style i.e. "active experimentation".

3. There is a negative correlation among the perception of self and achievement motivation of the talented speech and hearing impaired children.

The findings nos. 2 and 3 support to reject the hypotheses that "there is a positive correlation among perception of self and learning styles: perception of self and achievement motivation of the talented speech and hearing impaired children.

Regression Equations and Their Analysis

I. Talented Orthopaedically Impaired Children

1. Prediction of teacher's perception of the talented orthopaedically impaired children could be made on the basis of their preferred learning style and achievement motivation conjointly.
2. Prediction of perception of self of the talented orthopaedically impaired children could be made on the basis of the group's preferred "learning style" (single variable); and "achievement motivation" conjointly. This finding supports to uphold the hypothesis that prediction of perception of self of the talented orthopaedically impaired children could be made on the basis of their preferred learning style.

II. Talented Visually Impaired Children

1. Prediction of "teacher's perception" of the talented visually impaired children could be made on the basis of group's "achievement motivation" (single) and "task related motivation" and preferred "learning styles" (conjointly).
2. Prediction of perception of self of the talented visually impaired children could not be made on the basis of the group's preferred learning style i.e. "active experimentation" and "achievement motivation". Thus, the hypothesis that perception of self of the talented visually impaired children could be made on the basis of their learning styles and achievement motivation is rejected.

III. Talented Speech and Hearing Impaired Children

1. "Teacher's perception of the talented speech and hearing impaired children could be predicted only on the basis of their preferred learning style i.e. "active experimentation".

2. Prediction of "perception of self" of the talented speech and hearing impaired children could be made on the basis of the group's second preferred learning style i.e. "reflective observation" and "achievement motivation" conjointly. This finding supports to uphold the hypothesis that "prediction of perception of self of the talented speech and hearing impaired children could be made on the basis of their preferred learning style and achievement motivation".

Having analysed the data, the investigator is able to state that the framed objectives of the present study have been achieved in the following manner:

Objective No. 1: To identify the talented orthopaedically impaired, visually impaired and speech and hearing impaired children.

Thirty-six talented exceptional children, twelve catering to each group were identified. This shows that the objective no. 1 is fulfilled.

Objective No. 2: To explore the perception of self, learning styles and motivational characteristics of the talented orthopaedically impaired, visually impaired and speech and hearing impaired children.

The findings of the study show that each of the three categories of talented exceptional children possess low perception of self. The predominant learning style of the talented orthopaedically impaired and visually impaired children are "active experimentation" and "reflective observation" respectively. The talented speech and hearing impaired children possess two preferred learning styles, namely, "active experimentation" and "reflective observation". The talented orthopaedically impaired and speech and hearing impaired children possess low achievement motivation while the talented visually impaired children possess moderate achievement motivation.

Based on the above-said findings it could be said that the objective no. 2 is achieved.

Objective No. 3: To explore the differences among each of the three groups of talented exceptional children on the above-said three variables.

The talented orthopaedically impaired children differ significantly from the talented visually impaired children on perception of self, active experimentation learning style and on achievement motivation. Significant group differences between the talented orthopaedically impaired and speech and hearing impaired children have been found on "perception of self" and on "abstract conceptualization" learning style. The talented speech and hearing impaired and visually impaired children differ significantly on "active experimentation" learning style and on "achievement motivation".

The above said findings support to state that the objective no. 3 is fulfilled.

Objective No. 4: To find out, intercorrelations among perception of self, learning styles and motivational characteristics of each of the three groups of talented exceptional children.

Correlational studies depict that perception of self of the talented orthopaedically impaired children correlates positively with the group's preferred learning style and with achievement motivation. In case of the talented visually impaired children, perception of self of the group correlates positively with the group's preferred learning style and correlates negatively with the group's achievement motivation. Perception of self of the talented speech and hearing impaired children correlates negatively with the group's preferred learning style and with achievement motivation.

Based on the above-said findings it could be said that the objective no. 4 is achieved.

Objective No. 5: To find out strength of predictability of teacher's perception of each of the three groups of talented exceptional children on the basis of perception of self, learning styles and motivational characteristics.

It has been found that prediction of teacher's perception of the talented orthopaedically impaired, visually impaired and speech and hearing impaired children could be made on the basis of the concerned group's preferred learning style and achievement motivation; motivational characteristics and preferred learning style; and preferred learning style respectively. Thus, it could be said that the objective no. 5 is achieved.

Objective No. 6: To find out strength of predictability of perception of self of each of the three groups of talented exceptional children on the basis of learning styles and motivational characteristics.

Regression analysis shows that prediction of perception of self of the talented orthopaedically impaired children could be made on the basis of the group's preferred learning style and achievement motivation conjointly. Perception of self of the talented visually impaired children could not be made on the basis of the group's preferred learning style and achievement motivation, while in case of the talented speech and hearing impaired children prediction of perception of self could be made on the basis of the group's preferred learning style and achievement motivation.

The above-said findings support to state that the objective no. 6 is fulfilled.

The analysis and interpretation of data done through both quantitative and qualitative descriptions helped the investigator in establishing the status of the talented orthopaedically impaired, visually impaired and speech and hearing impaired children on "perception of self", "learning styles" and "motivational characteristics". It also helped in achieving the framed objectives and in testing the formulated hypotheses of the study. Besides this, it also documented the findings of the study.

Based on the findings of the study, obtained through both quantitative and qualitative description of data, the investigator drew conclusions. Conclusions, implications and suggestions of the study have been presented in the next chapter.

6

Conclusions, Implications and Suggestions

Logic tells us that the earlier we identify the potentially gifted and talented physically challenged children and provide them with programming to nurture their abilities, the greater will be their chances of fully actualizing their potential. It is not surprising that we are lagging even further behind in developing appropriate procedures for identifying and programming for the gifted and talented children with handicapping conditions. There is a need to foster a commitment to develop procedures for improving the lives of this sub-group of children by restructuring the existing schemes and deriving new directions. Few such directions are placed in this chapter based on findings of the present study, which would help explore the possibilities of future research in the field of gifted and talented physically challenged children and their education.

In the present study the talented exceptional children manifested variance as well as similarities in their self-perceptions, learning styles, and motivational characteristics. Because of gross individual differences and small sample size, it is difficult to make generalizations for educational objectives and their implementation. The study through different stages of investigations reached the following conclusions which are the result of statistical as well as qualitative analysis of data collected systematically.

Conclusions

1. The researcher through his interviews with the teachers of the physically challenged children came to know that they

are hardly aware of the fact that these children would possess potential gifts/talents. Teachers of the children with handicapping conditions have little knowledge regarding identification of talents/gifts among these children. Contrary to opinion of many, it is possible to identify indicators of above average abilities and talents among the physically challenged children. It is felt that teachers can effectively identify potentially gifted and talented exceptional children if they are provided with an instrument which will guide them in observing children's behaviour in classroom settings and outside.

2. Only 36 talented ones could be identified from a sample of 600 physically challenged children. The prevalence of the talented exceptional children as found in the present study is reported to be 6%.

3. The talented exceptional children are a special category and distinct from their other handicapped peers. Each of the three categories of exceptional children, though show variation, have low perception of self. They possess low perception of their abilities, strengths, feelings, attitudes, aspirations and goals of life. However, the talented orthopaedically impaired, talented visually impaired and the talented speech and hearing impaired children are quite sure about their future success and failure.

4. Among the three groups, the talented orthopaedically impaired children have higher "self" than both the talented visually impaired and talented speech and hearing impaired children. This may be due to the fact that the talented orthopaedically impaired children are advanced in receiving stimuli through vision and hearing compared to other two groups, which helps a lot in developing self-concept. On the other hand, lack of vision for the talented visually impaired children and lack of verbal communicating ability for the talented speech and hearing impaired children might have produced low perception of self. However, the talented visually impaired and the talented speech and hearing impaired children do not vary significantly to each other on self-perception. This implies that neither of the group is superior to the other on "perception of self".

5. The talented orthopaedically impaired, talented visually impaired and the talented speech and hearing impaired children possess high "academic self". They share many commonalities among themselves. These children are found to be more academically oriented and have clear perception of their academic abilities. They are regular to schools and are fully sincere towards academic endeavours. They possess rapid learning ability. They are curious to explore the environment. They are good in problem solving. They show willingness to take risk for the purpose of attainment of future goals. They are hard working. They advocate for the prevalence of discipline and impartial judgment. They take part in various cocurricular activities. They enjoy the company of their handicapped peers. They possess a keen sense of humour. They are capable of capitalising on personal strength and abilities.

6. On academic self, among the three groups, the talented orthopaedically impaired children are found superior to the talented visually impaired children. No group variation is found between the talented visually impaired and the talented speech and hearing impaired children.

7. The talented orthopaedically impaired, talented visually impaired and the talented speech and hearing impaired children have low social self. These children appear to struggle with self acceptance. They have feelings of social discomfort and shame. They experience interprersonal difficulties with their normal peers. They are not able to fit themselves into the mainstream and are not advanced in social relations. They find it difficult in meeting people in social gatherings and in other activities. They have a limited friend circle. They do not want to be disturbed by others. They love the company of similar handicapped peers only. However, among the three groups only the talented orthopaedically impaired children vary to the talented speech and hearing impaired children on social self. The previous group is found superior to the latter one. No group variation is found between the talented orthopaedically impaired and the talented visually impaired children and between the talented visually impaired and talented speech and hearing impaired children.

The contributing factors for developing low perception of social self of the talented orthopaedically impaired, talented visually impaired and the talented speech and hearing impaired children could be many.

For the talented visually impaired children this may be due to the lack of vision. Visual experiences have a long distance object quality which are unique among all human senses. This permits the control of the environment and the self. Thus lack of sight causes a detachment from the physical and to some extent from the social environment. Like vision, social development also depends on communication. Social interaction by definition is the communication of ideas between two or more people. For the talented speech and hearing impaired children as they are frequently cut off from communicating with the population at large, therefore, these children grow up in relative isolation and experience more problems of living in the society.

Like vision and language, physical ability is the prerequisite by which one can learn about himself. For the talented orthopaedically impaired children, an existing defect and impaired physique develop a sense of inferiority complex which make them experience greater difficulty in facing socially accepted points of reference. They find it difficult to grow up with the expectation based on what the normal children around them do and work to achieve. As a result these children manifest a low perception of their social traits.

8. The talented orthopaedically impaired, the talented visually impaired and the talented speech and hearing impaired children possess low physical self. Among the three groups no group variation is found on physical self. Each of the three categories of the talented exceptional children more or less equally perceive their physical strength, worth and abilities. These children possess clear perception of their physical abilities and disabilities. The talented orthopaedically impaired children consider physical disability as a stigma with regard to doing of skilled labours. The talented visually impaired children do not consider blindness as a hurdle in achieving goals of life. They reveal that they would be more perfect in their jobs if they were to see the world around them. The talented speech and hearing impaired children though

have low physical self, possess indifferent opinions about their physical abilities and strengths.

9. Each of the three categories of talented exceptional children show different preferences for choosing their learning styles. The predominant learning style of the talented orthopaedically impaired children is found to be "active experimentation" and for the talented visually impaired children it is "reflective observation". The talented speech and hearing impaired children have two preferred learning styles, namely, 'active experimentation" and "reflective observation".

10. The talented orthopaedically impaired children at the time of learning emphasize on practical applications as opposed to reflective understanding or, say, on doing as opposed to observing. They enjoy and are good at getting things accomplished. They are willing to take some risk to achieve their learning objectives and want to see the learning results. They also value having an impact and influence on the environment around them during learning.

11. The talented visually impaired children during learning a task emphasise on understanding as opposed to practical application, a concern with what is true or how things happen as opposed to what is practical an emphasis on reflection as opposed to action. They focus on understanding the meaning of ideas and situations by carefully observing and impartially describing them. They have poor abstract conceptualisation ability. They enjoy thinking about the meaning of situations and ideas and are good at seeing their implications. They like to rely on their own thoughts and feelings to form opinions. They value patience, impartially and considered thoughtful judgement.

12. The talented speech and hearing impaired children have two preferred learning styles i.e. "active experimentation" and "reflective observation". They employ these two learning styles depending on the nature of the learning tasks. They emphasise both on practical application as well as on reflective understanding during learning. These children are poor in abstract conceptualisation. They show willingness to achieve their learning objectives by doing hard work. They

understand the meaning of ideas by carefully observing and doing. They like to rely on their own thoughts and feelings to form opinions. They want to see their learning outcomes.

13. Each of the three categories of talented exceptional children express their boredom in the monotonous classroom activities and desire changes in the system.

14. It is found that the talented orthopaedically impaired and the talented speech and hearing impaired children possess low motivation to achieve. They have scored low on achievement motivation. They express less optimistic views about their future success. They consider their physical disabilities as barrier in achieving life's goals.

15. The talented visually impaired children have moderate motivation to achieve. They are quite optimistic about their future success. They possess clear perception of their abilities. They are willing to work hard in order to achieve life's goals.

16. Teacher's perception of the talented orthopaedically impaired children correlates positively with the groups "academic self", "physical self" and with group's most preferred learning style i.e. "active experimentation". It indicates that teacher's perception of the group is dependent on the group's "academic self" and preferred learning style. Teacher's perception of the group correlates negatively with the group's achievement motivation. This reflects that "achievement motivation" of the group is negatively related to the group's teacher's perception.

17. A high positive significant correlation is found between "perception of self" and preferred learning style i.e. "active experimentation", and a low positive correlation is found between "perception of self" and "achievement motivation" of the talented orthopaedically impaired children. It reflects that perception of self of the talented orthopaedically impaired children is highly affective on the group's preferred earning style and less affective on the group's achievement motivation.

18. Teacher's perception of the talented visually impaired children correlates negatively with perception of self and preferred learning style i.e. "reflective observation" and

correlates positively with achievement motivation of the group. This reflects that achievement motivation of the talented visually impaired children highly affect the group's achievement motivation. Teacher's perception of the group is not dependent on the group's perception of self and preferred learning style.

19. Perception of self of the talented visually impaired children shows positive correlation with preferred learning style and negative correlation with achievement motivation of the group. This indicates that achievement motivation of the group does not affect perception of self of the group and the group's most preferred learning style has low positive affect on the perception of self of the group.

20. Teacher's perception of the talented speech and hearing impaired children correlates negatively with the group's "perception of self", preferred "learning style", and "achievement motivation". This shows that teacher's perception of the group is not dependent on the group's perception of self, preferred learning style and achievement motivation.

21. Perception of self of the talented speech and hearing impaired children correlates positively with preferred learning style and correlates negatively with the group's achievement motivation. It indicates that achievement motivation of the group does not affect the group's perception of self.

22. Prediction of teacher's perception of the talented orthopaedically impaired children could be made on the basis of the group's "task related motivation".

23. Predication of perception of self of the talented orthopaedically impaired children could be made on the basis of group's most preferred learning style i.e. "active experimentation".

24. Teacher's perception of the talented visually impaired children could be predicated on the basis of group's motivational characteristics (both achievement motivation and task related motivation).

25. Prediction of perception of self of the talented visually impaired children could not be made on the basis of the group's preferred learning style and achievement motivation.

26. Teacher's perception of the talented speech and hearing impaired children could be predicted on the basis of group's most preferred learning style i.e. "active experimentation".
27. Prediction of "perception of self" of the talented speech and learning impaired children could be made on the basis of the group's most preferred learning style i.e. "active experimentation" and "achievement motivation".

Educational Implications

1. The study will help the special educators in identifying the orthopaedically impaired, visually impaired and speech and hearing impaired children with potential gifts/talents.
2. Knowledge of self of the talented exceptional children will enable the teachers, counsellors, psychologists and other related professionals in the field in gaining deeper understanding of the characteristics of these children. This will help in providing proper guidance and counselling keeping in view the positive self-concept development of these children.
3. Understanding of the learning style preferences of such children will enable the teachers in designing appropriate and proper educational programmes, structuring the learning environment and framing teaching strategies for their education. This will help in restricting the unnecessary wastage of precious manpower on the part of learners as well as teachers.
4. An insight into the motivational characteristics of the talented exceptional children will help the educators in framing the curricular and co-curricular activities accordingly. This will help in nurturing the motivational dispositions of these children.

Suggestions for Teacher and Parents

The findings of the present study lead to the following suggestions for the teachers and parents of the talented exceptional children:

(i) The talented orthopaedically impaired, visually impaired and speech and hearing impaired children should be identified as early as possible.

(ii) Professionals of special education like special educators, psychologists, counsellors and social workers should work in close cooperation along with the parents in order to identify the talented psysically challenged children and nurture their potential gifts and talents.

(iii) Special educators need to be familiar with the characteristics of giftedness and talent of the physically challenged children.

(iv) Information from various sources like parents, peers and teachers must be collected and both formal and informal assessment procedures should be adopted in identifying the talented exceptional children.

(v) Teachers of the physically challenged children should be provided with identifying tools that would guide them in observing behaviours of the physically challenged children in different situations.

(vi) Parents should be given adequate knowledge to help them to search potential gift and talent of their physically challenged children during their early childhood.

(vii) The talented physically challenged children should be properly studied and their multidimensional needs are to be explained along with difficulties they encounter both at home and in school which hinder their academic achievement as well as socialization.

(viii) The talented exceptional children should not be left out because of their handicapness; rather be encouraged to take part in different activities both in school, home and society.

(ix) Positive environment should be provided for the right development of self-concept of these children. Programmes in school should be organised not only to help these children to achieve but also to help them to appreciate the worth of their achievements. Achievement of these children should be never compared with that of their non-handicapped peers.

(x) The talented physically challenged children should be given opportunity to take part in social activities with other bright or creative children in order to enrich their experiences.

(xi) These children must be encouraged to have open communications with their non-handicapped peers not only to develop social skills and social relations but also to minimise their feeling of social rejection. Special coaching should be given in order to strengthen their social adaptive skills.

(xii) The talented exceptional children must be provided with appropriate learning situations so that they learn best by their preferred learning styles.

(xiii) They should be male independent to get learning experiences and to take part in small group activities in which they can serve as leaders and as equal participants.

(xiv) Variety of learning experiences through different academic activities should be provided to these children so that they do not express their boredom with the existing routine works.

(xv) Due to limited sensory inputs these children generally manifest poor abstract thinking skills. Educational programmes should focus on the development of skills like critical thinking, creativity, problem solving, analysing and synthesizing of ideas, ability to evaluate and generalize.

(xvi) Specialized extra coaching should be provided by individualized educational programmes with timely guidance to these children.

(xvii) Parents of the talented physically challenged children must deal with their child's special needs related to the handicap as well as attend to his/her gift or talent.

(xviii) Parents must be educated enough to develop sensory awareness, knowledge, vocabulary and learning

skills of the talented exceptional children. This would enable these children to explore their environment at an early age at home.

(xix) Parents should be made aware enough how to nurture potential gift or talent or how to help the talented physically challenged children blossom fully and effectively.

(xx) Parents of the talented physically challenged children should not restrict them in interacting with their non-handicapped peers. These children rather should be encouraged by their parents to integrate into the social mainstream in the most possible way in order to develop self confidence, social intimacy and positive self-concept.

(xxi) Focus should be given on balanced growth of achievement motivation of the talented exceptional children both by teachers and parents.

(xxii) In schools there should be facilities available in terms of use of technological devices in order to make the teaching learning process of the talented exceptional children an effective one.

(xxiii) Parents must ensure that continuity in the educational programmes available in the schools for the talented physically challenged children.

(xxiv) Teacher training programmes should provide training packages to the would-be teachers of the physically challenged children in order to enable them identify the talented exceptional children as well as nurture their potential gift and talent.

Limitations

1. The present study was conducted in Delhi focusing only on four special schools. The physically challenged children studying in regular schools as well as in mainstreamed classes were not dealt with.
2. Special schools outside Delhi were excluded from the present study for the purpose of sample selection.

3. The study did not cover a large number of special schools both in Delhi and outside. As a result, only 36 talented exceptional children were identified, which comprised the final sample of the study.
4. The findings of the study could not be considered for the purpose of their wider, universal generalisations and applications because of its small sample size.
5. The standardized psychological tools, if available, could and should have been used to ensure unbiased identification of the talented orthopaedically impaired, visually impaired, and speech and hearing impaired children.
6. Some more psychological variables like aptitudes, interest and personality were not studied. Study of these variables would be helpful in developing profiles of the talented exceptional children.

Suggestion for Further Study

1. Study should be conducted for the development of standardized tools for the purpose of identification of the gifted and/or talented children with handicapping conditions.
2. Study should be conducted in a larger number of special schools comprising of large sample size.
3. The mainstreamed orthopaedically impaired, visually impaired, and speech and hearing impaired children should be studied for the purpose of talent identification.
4. Variables other than those taken in the present study like aptitudes, interest, personality should be studied, so as to find various characteristics of these children.
5. Case study approach should be employed in order to have broaden knowledge about various characteristics of the gifted/talented children with handicapping conditions.

Bibliography

1. Alexander, Patricia, A and Muia, Joseph, A (1982): *Gifted Education.* London, Aspen Systems Corporation.

2. Allinson, C.W. and Hayes, J. (1990): "Validity of the Learning Styles Questionnaire". *Psychological Reports,* 67, 859-866.

3. Atkinson, C.W. (1988): "Reliability of the Learning Style Inventory-1985", *Psychological Report,* 62, 755-758.

4. Atkinson, J.W. (1966): *An Introduction to Motivation.* Toronto, D. Van Nostrand Company, INC.

5. Atkinson, J.W. (1983): *Personality, Motivation and Action.* New York, Praeger.

6. Baker, J.D., Conroy, J.M., and Alpert, C.C. (1990): Learning Style Analysis—A Commentary, *Perceptual and Motor Skills,* 70, 305-306.

7. Bandura, A. (1989): "Regulation of cognitive process through perceived self efficacy", *Developmental Psychology,* 25, 5, 729-735.

8. Bandura, A. (1994): Self Esteem, In R.J. Corsini (Eds.) *Encyclopedia of Psychology* (II ED.), New York, John Willey and Sons, pp. 369-370.

9. Bandura, Albert and Walters, Richard. H. (1963): *"Social Learning and Personality Development"*, New York, Holt, Rinehart and Winston.

10. Bandura, B.M. (1984); "The general academic self-concept normological network: A review of construct validation research", *Review of Educational Research,* 54, 3, 427-456.

11. Bear, George G.; Juvonen, Jaona and Mclnerney, Frances (1993): "Self-perceptions and Peer relations of boys with and boys without learning disabilities in an integrated setting", *Learning Disabilities Quarterly,* Vol. 16(2), 127-136.

12. Belts, George T, and Neihart, Maureen (1988): Profiles of Gifted and Talented; *Gifted Child Quarterly,* 32(2), 248-253.

13. Besemer, Susan and Quin, Karen, O. (1986): Analyzing Creative Products: Refinement and test of judging instrument. *The Journal of Creative Behaviour* 20(2), Second Quarter, 115-125.

14. Besemer, Susan, P. and Treffinger, Donald J. (1981): "Analysis of Creative Products" Review and Synthesis; *The Journal of Creative Behaviour,* 15(3), Third Quarter, 158-177.

15. Blough, Lisa K., Ritten House, Robert K. and Daner, Jess (1999): "Identification of gifted deaf children, A complex but critical educational process", *Perceptual and Motor Skills,* Vol. 89(1), 219-221.

16. Brantlinger, E.A. and Guskin, S.L. (1987): Ethno-cultural and Social Psychological Effects on Learning Characteristics of Handicapped Children. In M.C. Wang, M.C. Reynolds, and H.J. Walberg (Eds.), *Handbook of Special Education: Research and Practice:* Vol. 1, Learner characteristics and adoptive education (pp 7-34), Oxford, England, Pergamon.

17. Brim, Orville. G. (Jr.) (1966): *"Socialization through the life cycle"*, New York: John Wiley and Sons.

18. Brown, M.S. and Hayden, R.R. (1989): "Learning Style—Liberal Arts and Technical Training: What is the difference?" *Psychological Reports,* 64, 507-518.

19. Burns, Mary T. (1988): Music as a tool for Enhancing Creativity, *The Journal of Creative Behaviour,* 22(1), 62-69.

20. Campbell. J.D. (1990): "Self esteem and clarity of the self-concept", *Journal of Personality and Social Psychology,* 59, 538-49.

21. Campbell, J.D., Trapnel, P.D., Keive, S.J., Katz, I.M., Lavelee, L.F. and Lehman, D.R. (1996); "Self-Concept Clarity: Measurement, Personality Correlates, and Cultural Boundaries", *Journal of Personality and Social Psychology,* 70: 141-56

22. Carbo, Marie (1983): "Research in reading and learning style: Implications for exceptional children", *Exceptional Children,* Vol. 49(6), 486-494.

23. Cartledge, Gwendolyn; Cochran, Lessie and Paul, Peter (1996); "Social Skill self assessments by adolescents with hearing impairment in residential and public schools", *Remedial and Special Education,* Vol. 17(1), 30-36.

24. Chapman, James, W. (1988): Cognitive-Motivational Characteristics and Academic Achievement of Learning Disabled Children: A longitudinal Study; *Journal of Educational Psychology.* 88(3), 357-365.

25. Chon, L.K.S. (1988): The Perceived Competence of Intellectually Talented Students, *Gifted Child Quarterly,* 32, 310-315.

26. Clark, Barbara (1992): *"Growing up gifted"*, New York, Merril, an imprint of MacMillan Publishing Company.

27. Colangelo, N. and Kerr, B.A. (1990): "Extreme Academic Talent: Profiles of Perfect Scorers", *Journal of Educational Psychology*, 82(3), 404-409.

28. Colangelo, Nicholas and Davis, Gary A. (1991); *Handbook of Gifted Education;* Boston, Allyn and Bacon.

29. Collan, Victor, J. and John Debra. S.F. (1984): Self and other perceptions of Urban and Rural Australian Aboriginal and White Youth; *The Journal of Creative Behaviour*, 123, Second half, 179-185.

30. Cooley, E; Ayres, R. and Dann, C. (1990): "Self-concept, Attribution, and Persistence in Learning-Disabled students", *The Journal of School Psychology*, 28, 153-163.

31. Cooley, Eric. J. and Ayres, Robert. R. (1988): Self-concept and Success-failure Attributions of non-handicapped students and Students with Learning Disabilities; *Journal of Learning Disabilities*, 21(3), 174-178.

32. Corte, E.D.; Lodewijks, H.; Parmentier, R. and Span, P. (1987): *Learning and Instruction;* Great Britain, Pergamon Press. pp. 133-145.

33. Crocker, Alison D. and Orr, R. Robert (1996): "Social behaviours of children with visual impairments enrolled in preschool programmes", *Exceptional Children*, 62(5), 451-462.

34. Curry, L. (1991): Learning styles Development in Continuing Education for Physicians. In M.L. Languis, J.J. Buffer, Jr.; D.J. Martin, and P.J. Naour (Eds), *Cognitive Science Contributions of Educational Practice*, pp. 396-403.

35. Davis, G.A. and Rimm, S.B. (1994). *Education of the Gifted and Talented*, Boston, Allyn and Bacon.

36. Dececco, John, P. and Crawford, William (1988): *The Psychology of Learning Instruction, Educational Psychology*, New Delhi, Printice Hall of India Pvt. Ltd.

37. Dillon, Ronna. F and Schmeck, Ronald. R. (1983). *Individual Differences in Cognition;* Vol. 1, New York, Academic Press, pp. 233-274.

38. Driscoll, M.P. (1994): *"Psychology of Learning for Instruction"*. Boston, Allyn and Bacon, pp. 293-295.

39. Dunn, R.; Giannitti, M.C.; Murray, J.B.; Rossi, I.; Geisert, G. and Quinn. P. (1990): "Grouping students for Instruction: Effects of

Learning Styles on Achievement and Attiudes", *The Journal of Social Psychology*, 130(4), 485-494.

40. Dunn, Rita. (1983): "Learning style and it's relation to exceptionality at both ends of the spectrum", *Exceptional Children*, Vol. 49(6), 496-506.

41. Emanuelsson, I and Persson, B. (1997): "Who is considered to be in need of special education; why, how and by whom?" *European Journal of Special Needs Education*, 12, 2, 127-136.

42. Entwistle, Noel. J. (1987): *Understanding Classroom Learning*, London, Hodder and Stoughton.

43. Entwistle, Noel. J. and Ramsden, Paul (1982): Understanding Students Learning; New York, Nicholas Publishing Company, pp. 1-28.

44. Entwistte, N.J. (1981): *Styles of Learning and Teaching*, New York, Wiley.

45. Eson, M.E. (1972): *Psychological Foundations of Education*, New York, Holt, Rinehart and Winston.

46. Eysenck, M.W. (1994): *The Black Well Dictionary of Cognitive Psychology*. Oxford, U.K. Black Well Publishers.

47. Farmer, Thomas W., Rodkin, Philip C., Pearl, Ruth and Van Acker, Richard (1999): "Teacher-assessed behavioural configurations, peer assessments and self-concepts of elementary students with mild disabilities". *Journal of Special Education*, 1999 (Sum) Vol. 33(2), 66-80.

48. Ferrell, Barbara G. (1983): A Factor Analytic Comparison of Four Learning-Styles Instruments; *Journal of Educational Psychology*, 75(1), 33-39.

49. Flimian, Michael J.; Faford, Mary-Beth. and Howell, K.W. (1988): *A Teacher's Guide to Human Resources in Special Education*, Boston, Allyn and Bacon, Inc.

50. Fransson, A. (1977): On Qualitative Differences in Learning; IV-Effects of Intrinsic Motivation and Extrinsic Test Anxiety on Process and Outcome; *British Journal of Educational Psychology*, 47, 244-257.

51. Freeman, J. (1983): Emotional Problems of the Gifted Child. *Journal of Child Psychology*, 24, 481-485.

52. Freeman, Joan. (1986): *"The Psychology of Gifted Children, Perspectives on Development and Education*, Chichostor, John Wiley and Sons.

53. Gagne', Francoys (1989), Peer Nominations as a Psychometric Instrument: Many Questions Asked but Few Answered. *Gifted Child Quarterly*, 33(2), 53-58.

54. Gagne', Francoys, (1991), Towards a Differentiated Model of Giftedness and Talent. In Nicholas Colongelo and Gary A. Davis (Eds), *Handbook of Gifted Education*, Boston, Allyn and Bacon, pp. 65-78.

55. Gallagher, J.J. (1985): *Teaching the Gifted Child.* Newton, M.A. Allyn and Bacon.

56. Gartner, A. and Lipskey, D.K. (1989): "New Conceptualisations for Special Education", *European Journal of Special Needs Education,* 4(1), 16-21.

57. Gartnet, A. and Lipsky, D.K. (1987): "Beyond Special Education: Towards a Quality system for all Students", *Harvard Educational Review,* 57(4), 379-395.

58. Gilmer, B.H. (1970): *Psychology,* New York, Harper International Edition.

59. Ginter, Earl. J.; Scalise, Joseph, Brown; Steve, and Ripley, William. (1989): Perceptual Learning Styles: Their Link to Academic Performance, Sex, Age, and Academic Standing; *Perceptual and Motor Skills,* 68, 1091-1094.

60. Graham, S. and Golan, S. (1991): Motivational Influences on Cognition: Task Involvement, Ego Involvement, and Depth of Information Processing, *Journal of Educational Psychology,* 83(2), 187-194.

61. Green, D.W.; Snell, J.C.; and Parimanath, A.R. (1990): "Learning Styles in Assessment of Students", *Perceptual and Motor Skills,* 70, 363-369.

62. Gregg, G.S. (1991); *Self Representation:* Life Narrative Studies in Identity and Ideology, New York: Green Wood Press.

63. Griggs, Shirely. A, (1984); "Counseling the gifted and talented based on learning styles", *Exceptional Children,* Vol. 50(5), 429-432.

64. Grolnick, Wedny S. and Ryn, Richard M. (1990): Self-perceptions, Motivation and Adjustment in Children with Learning Disabilities", *Journal of Learning Disabilities,* Vol. 23(3). 177-184.

65. Gronmo, Siv Johanne and Augestad, Liv Berit (2000): *Journal of Visual Impairment and Blindness,* Vol. 94(8); 522-527.

66. Guskin, Samuel L., Peng, Chao-Ying J., Jabbari, Massoumeh (1988): Teacher's Perceptions of Giftedness, *Gifted Child Quarterly,* 32(1), 217-221.

67. Hallahan, Deniel P, and Kauffman, James M. (1991): *Exceptional Children: Introduction to Special Education;* Englewood Cliffs, New Jersey, Printice Hall.

68. Hamachek, D.E. (1971): *Encounters with the Self,* New York: Holt, Rinehart and Winston.

69. Hassett, J. and White, K.M. (1989): *Psychology in Perspective,* New York, Harper and Row Publishers, pp. 419-459.

70. Havighust, R.J. (1951): *Developmental Tasks and Education,* New York, Longman.

71. Hayden, Robert R. and Brown, Margery, S. (1985): Learning Styles and Correlates; *Psychological Reports,* 56, 243-246.

72. Heller, H.A.; Monks, F.J. and Passow, A.H. (1993): *International Handbook of Research and Development of Giftedness and Talent",* Oxford, Pergamon.

73. Heward, William L. and Orlansky, Michael. D. (1984): *Exceptional Children.* An Introductory Survey of Special Education, Columbus, Charles E. Merrill Publishing Company.

74. Hewitt, P.L. and Genest, Myles (1990): The Ideal Self: Schematic Processing of Perfectionistic Content in Dysphoric University Students, *Journal of Personality and Social Psychology,* 59(4), 802-808.

75. Hollingworth, L.S. (1926): *Gifted Children: Their Nature and Nurture,* New York, Macmillan.

76. Howell, K.W.; Kaplan, J.S. and Connell, C. Yo' (1979): *Evaluating Exceptional Children* (A test Analysis Approach): Columbus; Charles E.M. Merrill Publishing Company.

77. Hurley, John R. (1988): Interpersonal Correlates of Individuals' Discrepant Ratings by self and Peers; *The Journal of Social Psychology,* 128(5), 653-665.

78. Johnson, R.T., Johnson, David W. and Rynders, John (1981): Effect of cooperative, competitive and individualistic experiences on self esteem of handicapped and non-handicapped students, *Journal of Psychology,* 108, 1, 31-34.

79. Johnson, S. and Rayser, G. (1994): Identification of Young Gifted Children from Lower Income Families. *Gifted and Talented International,* 9(2), 62-68.

80. Johnes, P.M. and Robinson, N.M. (1985): *Psychology Development in Intellectually Gifted Children.* In F.D. Howowitz and M.O. Brien (Eds), *The Gifted and Talented: Developmental Perspectives.* Washington DC. American Psychological Association, pp. 149-195.

81. Jones, Thomas. W., Sowell, Virginia M., Jones, Julie. K. and Butler, Lester G. (1981): Changing Children's Perceptions of Handicapped People; *Exceptional Children,* 47(5), 365-368.

82. Jordan, Theresa J. (1981): Self-concepts, Motivation, and Academic Achievement of Balck Adolescents; *Journal of Educational Psychology*, 73(4), 509-517.

83. Karnes, F.A. and Wherry, J.N. (1981): Self-concepts of Gifted Students as measured by the Piers Harris Children's Self-concept scale. *Psychological Reports, 49(3), 903-906.*

84. Karnes, M.B. and Johnson, L.J. (1991): "Gifted Handicapped"; In Nicholas Colongelo, and Gary A. Davis (Eds), *Handbook of Gifted Education;* Boston, Allyn and Bacon, pp. 428-437.

85. Keating, D.P. (Ed.). (1976): *Intellectually Talent: Research and Development,* Baltimere, Md.: Johns Hopkins University Press.

86. Keen, E.(1975): *A Primer of Phenomenological Psychology,* New York, Holt, Rihehart and Winston.

87. Kelly, K.R. and Colangelo, N. (1984): Academic and Social Self-Concepts of gifted, general and special students, *Exceptional Children,* 50(6), 551-554.

88. Ketcham, B. and Syndeer, R.T. (1977): Self attitudes of the intellectually and socially advantaged student: Normative Study of the Piers Harris Children's Self-concept scale. *Psychological Reports,* 40, 111-116.

89. Kinster Janet; Haskett, Mary; White, Karen and Robbins, Frank (1987); "Perceived competence and self worth of learning disabled and normally achieving students", *Learning Disability Quarterly,* Vol. 10(1), 37-44.

90. Kirk, S.A. and Gallagher, J.J. (1983): *Educating Exceptional Children,* Boston, MA: Houghton Mifflin.

91. Kitano, Margie, K., Kirby, Darrel. F. (1986): *Gifted Education: "A Comprehensive View"*, Boston; Little, Brown and Company.

92. Kolb, D.A. (1984): *Experiential Learning: Experience as the Source of Learning and Development,* Englewood Cliffs, N.J.: Printice Hall.

93. Kolb, D.A., Rubin, I.M., Melntyre, J.M., (1974): Organizational Psychology. Englewood Cliffs, N.J., Printice Hall.

94. Lally, A. and LaBrant, L. (1951): *Experiences with Children Talented in the Arts.* In Witty, P. (Ed). The Gifted Child, New York: D.C. Heath.

95. Languis, M. L., Buffer (Jr.), J.J., Martin, D.J., Naour, Paul, J. (1991); *Cognitive Science, Contributions to Educational Practice,* Gordon and Breach Science Publishers, Philadelphia. 397-403.

96. Languis, M.L.; Buffer, J.J., Martin, D.J., Nauror, P.J. (1991): *Cognitive Science, Contribution to Educational Practice,* Melbourne, Gordon and Breach Science Publishers.

97. Lawrence, B. (1991): Self-concept formation and physical Handicap: Some Educational Implications for Integration. *Disability, Handicap and Society* 6(2), 139-145.

98. Lee, Motoko, Y. (1984): Judgements of Significant others and Self-concept of Students from Developing Nations; *The Journal of Social Psychology*, 122, 127-134.

99. Licht, Barbara. G. (1983): Cognitive-Motivational Factors that Contribute to the Achievement of Learning-Disabled Children; *Journal of Learning Disabilities*, 16(8), 483-489.

100. Lindsay, Geoff; Dockrell, Julie (2000); *British Journal of Educational Psychology*, 70, 583-601.

101. Loeb, R.C. and Jay. G. (1987): Self-concept in Gifted Children: Differential Impact in Boys and Girls. *Gifted Child Quarterly*, 31, 9-14.

102. Loeding, Barbara L. and Greenan, James P. (1999): "Relationship between self ratings by sensory impaired students and teacher's ratings of generalizable skills", *Journal of Visual Impairment and Blindness*, Vol. 93(11), 716-727.

103. Logan, Frank A., Ferraro, Douglas P. (1978): *Systematic Analysis of Learning and Motivation:* New York, John Wiley and Sons.

104. Loroux, J.A. (1988): Voices from the Classroom: Academic and Social Self-concepts of gifted adolescents, *Journal for the Education of the Gifted*, 113, 3-18.

105. Lyxell, Bjorn and Holmberg, Ingegerd (2000): *British Journal of Educational Psychology;* 70, 505-518.

106. Maag, John W. and Rutherford, Robert, B. (1986): "Perceived Social Competence of Behaviourally Disordered, Learning Disabled and Non-disabled Students", *Journal of Instructional Psychology*, Vol. 13(1), 10-18.

107. Maitra, Krishna (1983): *Gifted and Talented. A Developmental Perspective*, Delhi, Discovery Publishing House.

108. Maitra, Krishna (1996): *Parenting the Gifted*, Delhi, Discovery Publishing House.

109. Malpass, L.F., Hocutt, M.O., Martin, E.P. and Givens, P.R. (1965): *Human Behaviour, A program for self Instruction*, New York, McGraw Hill Book Company.

110. Marland, S.P. (1972): *Education of the Gifted and Talented: Report to the Congress of the United States by the Commissioner of Education*, Washington D.C., U.S. Government Printing Office.

111. Mccandles, B.R. (1967), *Children Behaviour and Development,* New York, Holt, Rinehart and Winston.

112. McDavin, J.W. and Harari, H. (1968): *Social Psychology, Individuals, Groups, Societies,* New York, Harper and Row, pp. 220-234.

113. Milicic, M. N. and Maria S. A. (1990): "Low Achievement: It's relation to selfesteem and Socio-metric Status in children in Elementary school students", *International Journal of Special Education,* 5(1), 39-49.

114. Minner, S. (1990): Teacher Evaluation of Case Descriptions of LD Gifted Children; *Gifted Child Quarterly,* 34(1) 37-39.

115. Monks, F.J. and Van Bostel, H.W. (1985): *Gifted Adolescents: A Developmental Perspective in the Psychology of Gifted Children* by Joan Freeman (Eds) John Wiley and Sons Ltd.

116. Norden, Kerstinetal (1981): Learning Processes and Personality Development in Deaf Children, *International Journal of Rehabilitation Research,* 4(3), 393-395.

117. Osborne, J.K. and Byrnes, D.A. (1990): Identifying Gifted and Talented Students in an Alternative Learning Centre, *Gifted Child Quarterly,* 34(1-4), 143-146.

118. Paris, Scott G. and Oka, Evelyn R. (1986); "Self regulated learning among exceptional children", *Exceptional Children,* Vol. 53(2), 103-108.

119. Pintrich, P.R. and Groot, E.V. (1990): "Motivational and Self Regulated Learning Components of Classroom Academic Performance", *Journal of Educational Psychology,* 82(2), 33-40.

120. Pritchard, M.C. (1951): "The Contribution of Letas, Holling Worth to the Study of Gifted Children". In P. Witty (Ed), *The Gifted Child,* New York: D.C. Heath.

121. Purkey, W.W.(1970): *Self-concept and School Achievement,* Englewood Cliffs, N.J.: Printice Hall.

122. Renick, Mari Jo, and Harter, Susan (1989): Impact of Social Comparisons on the Developing Self-perceptions of Learning Disabled Students; *Journal of Educational Psychology,* 81(4), 631-638.

123. Renzulli, Joseph S. (1991): The dream, the design, the destination, *Gifted Child Quarterly,* Vol. 35(2), 73-80.

124. Reynolds, C.L. and Kamphaus, R.W. (1990): *Handbook of Psychological and Educational Assessment of Children;* New York, The Guilford Press.

125. Richardson, A.G. (1993): Learning style and ability grouping in the high school system, Some Caribbean Findings, *Educational Research,* 35(1) Spring, 69-74.

126. Ross, A and Parker, M. (1980): Academic and Social Self-concepts of the Academically Gifted. *Exceptional Children*, 47(2), 6-10.

127. Ruthmann Howard R. and Cosden, Merith (1996); "The relationship between self-perception of learning disability and achievement, self-concept and social support". *Learning Disability Quarterly*, Vol. 18(3), 203-212.

128. Schirmer, Barbara R. (1985): "Mental imagery and their reading comprehension of deaf children", *Reading Research and Instruction*, 34(3), 177-188.

129. Schneider, Bary H., Clegg, Marjorie R., Byrne, Barbara M., Ledingham, Jane. E., Crombire, Gail (1989): Social Relations of Gifted Children as a function of age and School Program; *Journal of Educational Psychology*, 81(1), 48-56.

130. Shavelson, R.J., Hubner, J.J. and Stanton G.C. (1976): "Self-concept: Validation of construct interpretation", *Review of Educational Research*, 46, 3, 407-441.

131. Silverman, L.K. (1994): Gifted Children with Handicaps. In Garry A. Davis, and Sylvia B. Rimm. (Eds). *Education of the Gifted and Talented;* Boston, Allyn and Bacon, pp. 349-366.

132. Smith, D.S. and Nagle, R.J. (1995): Self-perceptions and Social Comparisons Among Children with L.D. *Journal of Learning Disability*, 28(6), 364-371.

133. Smith, Linda H. & Renzulli, Joseph S. (1984): "Learning style preferences: A practical approach for classroom teachers", *Theory into Practice*, Vol. 23(1), 44-50.

134. Smith, Robert M. and Neisworth, John. T. (1975): *The Exceptional Child.* A Functional Approach, New York, McGraw Hill Book Company.

135. Sole, Paul and Carey, Dorism (1995): "The sociometric status of students with disabilities in a full inclusion school", *Exceptional Children*, 62 (1), 6-19.

136. Spence, and Helmreich (1983): Achievement Related Motives and Behaviours. In J.T. Spence (Ed), *Achievement and Achievement Motives: Psychological and Sociological Approaches*, pp. 7-74.

137. Starko, A.J. and Schack, G.D. (1989): Perceived Need, Teachers Efficacy, and Teaching Strategies for the Gifted and Talented. *Gifted Child Quarterly*, 33(2), 118-122.

138. Steininger, Marion and Garcia, Luis, T. (1989): Causal Thinking in Self-Selected Stories about Self and Others; *The Journal of Social Psychology*, 129(1), 113-115.

139. Stensrud, R.H. (1994): Self-concept. In R.J. Corsini (Eds). *Encyclopedia of Psychology* (II Ed), New York, John Wiley and Sons, pp. 360-368.

140. Stern berg, R.J. (1986): A Triarchic Theory of Giftedness. In R.J. Sternberg and J.E. Davidson (Eds). *Conception of Giftedness* (pp. 223-243). New York: Cambridge University Press.

141. Stinson, Michael S., Whitmore, Kathleen and Kluwin, Thomas N. (1996): "Self-perceptions of social relationships in hearing impaired adolescents", *Journal of Educational Psychology*, 88(1), 132-143.

142. Stipek, Deborah, (1998): *"Motivation to Learn" From Theme to Practice*, Boston, Allyn and Bacon.

143. Sullivan, Harry Stack (1953): *The Inter-personal Theory of Psychiatry*, New York, W.W. Norton and Company.

144. Svensson, L. (1977): On Qualitative Differences in Learning: III Study Skill and Learning; *British Journal of Educational Psychology*, 47, 233-243.

145. Swanson, B. Marian and Willis, Diane, J. (1981): *"An Introduction to Special Education, Understanding Exceptional Children and Youth"*, Chicago, Road McNally College Publishing Company.

146. Tallmadge, G. Kasten, and Shearer, James. W. (1969): "Relationships among Learning Styles, Instructional Methods and the Nature of Learning Experiences", *Journal of Educational Psychology*, 60(3), 220-230.

147. Tannenbaum, A.J. (1983): *Gifted Children: Psychological and Educational Perspectives*, New York: Macmillan Publishing Co.

148. Taylor, Ronald. L. (1993): Assessment of Exceptional Students, Educational and Psychological Procedures. Boston, Allyn and Bacon pp. 77-142; 273-367.

149. Telford, Charles W. and Sawrey, James M. (1981): *The Exceptional Individual*, New Jersey, Printice Hall. Inc. Englewood Cliffs.

150. Treffinger, Donald. J. (1980): The Progress and Peril of Identifying Creative Talent Among Gifted and Talented Students; *The Journal of Creative Behaviour*, 14(1), First Quarter, 21-33.

151. Vaughn, S., Hogan A., Kouzenkanani, K. and Shapiro, S. (1990): "Peer Acceptance, Self-perceptions and Social Skills of Learning Disabled Students Prior to Identification, *Journal of Educational Psychology*, 82(1), 101-106.

152. Vernon, M.D. (1969): *Human Motivation;* Cambridge, Cambridge University Press, pp. 3-8 and 108-128.

153. Viernstein, H.C. and Hogan, R. (1974): Parental Personality Factors and Achievement Motivation in Talented Adolescents. *Journal of Youth and Adolescence.* 4(2), 183-190.

154. Waldron, Karen A., Saphire, Diane G. and Rosenblum, Sve. Ann (1987): *Learning Disabilities and Giftedness:* Identification Based on Self-concept, Behaviour, and Academic Patterns. 20(7), 422-427.

155. Wang. M.C., Reynolds, M.C. and Walberg, H.J. (1990): *Special Education Research and Practice Synthesis of Findings.* Oxford, England: Pergamon Press, pp. 1-27.

156. Wessells, M.G. (1982): *Cognitive Psychology;* New York, Harper and Row, Publishers, pp. 1-35.

157. Westman, A.S. (1993): Learning Styles are Content Specific and Probably Influenced by Content Areas Studied, *Psychological Reports,* 73, 512-514.

158. Whitmore, J.R. (1981): Gifted Children with handicapping Conditions, A New Frontier, *Exceptional Children,* 48, 2, 106-116.

159. Willcoxson, L. and Prosser, M. (1996): Kolb's Learning Style Inventory (1985): Preview and Further Study of Validity and Reliability, *British Journal of Educational Psychology,* 66, 247-257.

160. Witty, Paul. (1951): *The Gifted Child,* Boston: Heath.

161. Worchel, F., Little, V., and Alcala, J. (1990): "Self-perceptions of Depressed Children on Tasks of Cognitive Abilities, *Journal of School Psychology,* 28, 97-104.

162. Wu. Tien Wu, Ching-Chih Kuo, Joyce, Steeves (1992): *Giftedness: Growing up Gifted and Talented.* In Proceedings of the Second Asian Conference Giftedness published by Dept. of Special Education, National Taiwan Normal University, Taiwan.

163. Wylie, R.C. (1974): *The Self-Concept,* Vol. 1 (Rev.Ed), Lincoln: University of Nebreska Press.

164. Wylie, R.C. (1994): Self-Control, In R.J. Corsini (Eds), *Encyclopedia of Psychology* (II Ed), New York, John Wiley and Sons, 363-366.

165. Yewchuk, Carolyn and Lupart, J.L. (1993): Gifted Handicapped: "A Desultory Duality". In H.A. Heller, F.J. Monks, and A.H. Palsow (Eds). *International Handbook of Research and Development of Giftedness and Talent,* Oxford, Pergamon, pp. 709-722.

166. Yewchuck, Carolyn and R. and Bibby, Mary. A (1989): "The Handicapped Gifted Child: Problems of Identification and Programming", *Canadian Journal of Education,* Vol. 14(1), 102-108.

167. Yewchuk, Carolyn R. and Bibby, Mary A. (1989): "Identification of Giftedness in Severely and Profoundly Hearing Impaired Students". Gifted Students with Disabilities, *Roeper Review*, Vol. 12(1), 42-48.

168. Yong, F.L. and McIntyre, J.D. (1992): *Journal of Learning Disabilities*, 25, 2, 124-132.

Index